MONTVILLE TWP. PUBLIC LIBRARY
90 Horseneck Road
Montville, N.J. 07045

D0917206

0 1021 0078609 8

√8/07

UN LINE

973.3
Caso
Caso, Adolph.

America's Italian
 founding fathers /

Montville Twp. Public Library
90 Horseneck Road
Montville, N.J. 07045-9626

PLEASE DO NOT REMOVE CARDS
FROM POCKET
There will be a charge if
not returned with book.

GAYLORD

MONTVILLE TWP. PUBLIC LIBRARY

Montville, N.J. 07045

America's Italian Founding Fathers

Donated

by

Montville
UNICO

America's Italian Founding Fathers

By ADOLPH CASO

BOSTON
BRANDEN PRESS
PUBLISHERS

© Copyright, 1975, by Branden Press, Inc.
Printed in the United States of America
Library of Congress Catalog Card Number 75-11384
ISBN 0-8283-1610-4

TO MY MOTHER

45
1
2.00

CONTENTS

Preface

Beccaria's little book, *On Crimes and Punishments*, was so influential that many nations of Europe changed parts of their constitutions while the author was still alive. In America of the revolutionary period, the little book was more influential than any other single book, its spirit incorporated in documents such as the Declarations of Cause and of Independence, the Constitution, and the Bill of Rights. John Adams quoted from it as early as 1768; later, the same Adams quotes Beccaria in both English and in Italian. Jefferson made extensive usage of the book, as did many other prominent Americans of this period. It may be a surprise to many students and historians alike that Beccaria's little book was published in America long before any book of men such as Voltaire, Rousseau, and Montesquieu, to name just a few.

With the help of this book, our American forefathers were able to resolve issues such as the separation of church and state, the role of organized religions, the type and role of government, the role of the citizen, and of the Federation. Yet, many issues raised by Beccaria are still unresolved today. The religious issue, capital punishment, secret accusations, and many others are being discussed all over the country. In reading the old translation, we might re-discover another dimension of the 1770 decade as well as find answers or solutions to problems that are pressing the citizen, his society, and his government today.

That several prominent Italians played an important role in the development of the documents that constitute the American form of government has been a fact overlooked by such historians as Becker, Hazelton, Kimball, and Bailyn.

The serious student and scholar of American history may well ask why the name of Beccaria has been absent from our history books; we might even ask why there should be an

Italian translation of the same Declaration whose original, together with a transcribed form, is herewith published for the first time.

It is hoped, therefore, that with this book another aspect of American history will have come to light. More important, it is hoped that the little book, ON CRIMES AND PUNISHMENTS, will be as useful and as stimulating to us in these last thirty years of our second millennium in dealing with and resolving the issues already resolved by our forefathers.

America's Italian Founding Fathers

Chapter 1.

BECCARIA AND THE AMERICAN REVOLUTION

Cesare Beccaria's *Dei Delitti e Delle Pene* (On Crimes and Punishments) may have been the single most influential book of the second half of the eighteenth century, having influenced both Europeans and Americans of the Revolutionary period.

In connection with the American experience, it can be said without risking too much that this single book found more outright application in making and shaping the new nation than is otherwise believed. The Declaration of Causes of 1775 and that of Independence of 1776, together with the Constitution and the Bill of Rights, can be traced to Beccaria's book, not so much for that which deals specifically with criminal law, but for that which deals with the basic rights of man, with the relationships that ought to exist between man and man, between man and his society, and between man and his government.

In Beccaria's mind, man was the center of the entire human experience — his motto being: happiness to the greatest number of individuals. With the individual citizen placed above all other things, old and new governments had to assure the possibility of allowing the individual to achieve happiness.

It follows, then, that only through a sound system of laws can the citizen be assured of his happiness. Laws, therefore, have to be made to secure this goal, and those laws which do not accomplish the purpose or abridge unnecessarily the liberty of the citizen must be immediately repealed.

Laws need be written in the simplest language possible so the citizens can read and understand them, and be responsible only for those acts which are specifically stated by those laws.

Lawmakers should look to the future and pass laws according to the needs of changing times, repealing those which have

13

no bearing on the present generation. In any event, whenever an individual runs counter to the laws, be the offense civil or criminal, Beccaria upholds the Roman principle which is basic to our system: the individual is innocent until proven guilty; and that no individual can be punished or tortured, and no individual can be made to accuse himself in a court of law or in any other place. Furthermore, if an accusation against an individual, of whatever nature, cannot be made public, such accusation has to be considered null and void.

Secret accusations, therefore, are not admissable, nor should they be allowed in a free state. Likewise, capital punishment should not be practiced in a nation that at the same time lays claim to civility and humanity.

Religion, being an individual experience, has to remain such and free of compromise. It must not come into play as an entity within the structure of government; it must be separate from the government. But, that very government must guarantee and protect the right of the citizen to believe and to practice according to his religious disposition.

Governments that officially adhere to a given religion become, in the eyes of Beccaria, as tyrannical as organized religion, because human nature always aspires to superimpose one's own beliefs and practices on others. To avoid spiritual tyranny, Beccaria proclaims separation of church and state, with religion being practiced individually or socially and not as a mandate of the government.

It is not an understatement to say that Beccaria presented to our American forefathers certain ideas that allowed them to resolve serious problems and to establish a viable form of government. His spirit was very much alive in such men as John Adams, Thomas Jefferson, Thomas Paine, and others equally important. But his spirit is much more alive in the various doc-

14

uments establishing the guidelines for the new government, and in books and pamphlets such as *Common Sense* and *The Rights of Man*.

One of the first to quote directly from Beccaria's book was John Adams, who, as is commonly held, influenced the course of events of this country as one of its greatest constitutional lawyers. Together with his cousin Samuel, John Adams signed the Declaration of Independence; was the first Vice-President and the second President of the newly-formed nation. In 1791, during his term as Vice-President, he saw the Bill of Rights become part of the U. S. Constitution. He was also a member of the Continental Congress from 1774-1778. He was involved, therefore, in practically every important event that led to the shaping of the various documents of the U. S. government, being particularly instrumental in bringing about the Constitution, which as a document, still governs with the effectiveness that has seen no equal.

It is important to note that John Adams concerned himself as much with the rights of the single individual as in assuring to all men the protection of those rights, even if it meant going counter to popular sentiments and against his own interests. This was the conscious and definitive driving force behind John Adams, the same force that permeates the documents on which this country's government is founded.

This spirit may be reflected in the unpopular actions he willingly took in defense of Captain Preston in connection with the 1770 Boston Massacre.

The roots of Adams' defense are to be found in the case of Rex v. Samuel Quinn, Worcester Superior Court, September 1768, as a result of which "the Man was acquitted."

Some two years after the decision, during a trip he was taking to .Plymouth on Thursday, 28 June 1770, John Adams

15

recalls the trial of 1768: "I have received such Blessings and enjoyed such Tears of Transport — and there is no greater Pleasure, or Consolation!"

The individual responsible for this joyful outburst was Cesare Beccaria Bonesana of Milan, Italy, from whose book Adams took the passage:

> If, by supporting the Rights of Mankind, and of invincible Truth, I shall contribute to save from the Agonies of Death one unfortunate Victim of Tyranny, or of Ignorance, equally fatal; his Blessing and Tears of Transport, will be sufficient Consolation to me, for the Contempt of all Mankind. (*Essays on Crimes and Punishments.* Page 42. *The Adams Papers,* "Diary and Autobiography of John Adams," Vol I, The Belknap Press, Cambridge, Mass., 1961, pp. 352-54.)

Quoting directly from Beccaria in 1770 on an incident that occurred in 1768 must mean that Adams knew of the book as early as 1768. English editions had appeared in Dublin as early as 1767. What should also be said is that Beccaria's book inspired Adams' action as early as 1770 when he defended Captain Preston, a symbol of what Samuel Adams called the "horrid Massacre" of Boston which took place the evening of 5 March.

The soldiers of the Twenty-ninth Regiment were alleged to have massacred children, women, and men. To prove the "horrid Massacre," Samuel Adams obtained sworn statements from ninety-six witnesses in support of the prosecutors. In view of these things, and knowing of his cousin's feelings against the Englishmen, John Adams, together with Josiah Quincy, accepted to defend Captain Preston and his six soldiers. Aided by the testimony of Patrick Carr, John Adams was able to have Captain Preston and his men acquitted.

In his defense, John Adams frequently made reference to the ideas of Beccaria. According to Zobel (*The Boston Massacre*), when John Adams quoted directly from Beccaria, he had an electrifying effect on the jury. But the passage that culminated his eloquent defense was the passage he had included in his June 28, 1770 entry into his Diary.

Obviously, Beccaria did not make just a passing impression on John Adams. As late as July 1786 — some sixteen years after his defense of Captain Preston — Adams was to make another entry into his Diary, this time giving first the English translation of the Italian: "Every Act of Authority, of one Man over another for which there is not an absolute Necessity, is tyrannical," and then the original text: *"Le Pene che oltre passano la necessita di conservare il deposito della Salute publica, sono ingiuste di lor natura."*

Though the Italian text is not preserved today, we can at least know that Adams had an Italian edition, and that he might have even attempted to read it at one point or other.

In his entry of February — July 1780, for instance, he lists for July 7 as having paid to a certain Borzachini for two Italian Grammars and eleven lessons; on the following day, he paid a Mr. Molini for Baretti's Italian Dictionary, for Beccaria's *"Delliti (Delitti) e Pene,"* and for Buonmattei's *Grammatica.* Then, on July 27, he paid a Mr. Pechini "one Quarter" for his two sons — apparently for Italian lessons. And what may also be significant is that John Adams saw fit to bequeath Beccaria's book to one of his sons.

Although it is generally accepted that Beccaria was often quoted in connection with reforms of criminal law, his influences encompassed a wider experience of human government. "Every Act of Authority," as quoted by John Adams in July of 1786, "of one Man over another for which there is not an absolute Necessity, is tyrannical." The paragraph from which John Adams takes the quote comes at the end of Chapter II. The passage reads as follows:

17

Punishments meted out beyond the necessity to preserve the depositary of public health are, by their nature, unjust, as they are just when they make public security sacred and inviolable, thereby allowing the sovereign to preserve the greatest amount of liberty for his subjects.

Although the book *On Crimes and Punishments* may deal extensively with criminal law, Beccaria's message is wider in scope, as can be seen in the above short paragraph.

Beccaria hoped to establish a system of laws that might better serve all of humanity to achieve greater perfection and, therefore, greater happiness and utility.

He believed that this could be achieved through sound and just laws, that only through a responsible code of laws could men achieve maximum perfectibility as persons and as members of society.

Through the laws — only enough laws as necessary — could each man protect and be protected. Only through the laws could mankind save itself from returning to the state of primitive barbarism.

When in his, *The Ideological Origin of the American Revolution,* Bernard Bailyn states that in "pamphlet after pamphlet the American writers cited . . . Beccaria on the reform of criminal law," he is not altogether right because he restricts Beccaria's scope.

Beccaria is concerned with the overall betterment of human life. By restricting Beccaria to the reform of criminal law, Bailyn also limits the American writers by placing them in fixed categories of human experiences without considering that often the overlapping of these experiences may be more important.

Surely in Beccaria's case, when he makes of the laws the means to an end for mankind, he is not thinking of criminal laws only, though literally he does emphasize them. Thus, when John Adams quotes from Beccaria, "Every Act of Authority, of one

18

Man over another for which there is not an absolute Necessity, is tyrannical," he is surely not limiting himself to considerations of criminal laws; he is contemplating how mankind can govern itself through an Authority that must not be tyrannical at the same time.

"The Law Is King," exclaims Thomas Paine in his pamphlet, *Common Sense,* in a paragraph reminiscent of Beccaria's fervor:

> But where, says some, is the King of America? I'l tell you. Friend, he reigns above, and doth not make havoc of mankind like the Royal Brute of Britain. Yet that we may not appear to be defective even in earthly honors, let a day be solemnly set apart for proclaiming the charter; let it be brought forth placed on the divine law, the Word of God; let a crown be placed thereon, by which the world may know, that so far we approve of monarchy, that in America THE LAW IS KING. For as in absolute governments the King is law, so in free countries the law ought to be king; and there ought to be no other. But lest any ill use should afterwards arise, let the crown at the conclusion of the ceremony, be demolished, and scattered among the people whose right it is.

Thomas Paine, a native of England, published the blistering pamphlet in January of 1776. It is strange that in it Paine does not quote from any of Beccaria's works. In fact, he does not even mention Beccaria, but quotes from Beccaria's contemporary and follower — Giacinto Dragonetti (1738-1818).

In 1766, Dragonetti published anonymously, his *Delle virtu e dei premi* (Virtues and Rewards) which complements *Dei delitti e delle pene* of Beccaria published two years earlier.

Dragonetti's book — like that of Beccaria, which received praise and fortune as a result of Voltaire's demonstrated interest — also received praise from Diderot who, in turn, imitated Dragonetti's work. But though Paine refers to Dragonetti, what he says sounds more like the thoughts if not the language of Beccaria:

> Should any body of men be hereafter delegated for this or some similar purpose, I offer them the following extracts from that wise observer

19

of Governments, Dragonetti. "The science," says he, "of the Politician consists in fixing the true point of happiness and freedom. Those men would deserve the gratitude of ages, who should discover a mode of government that contained the greatest sum of individual happiness, with the least national expense." (Paine, *Common Sense*).

Practically the same ideas are expressed by Beccaria in his introduction:

The laws were never dictated by a clear and cold examiner of human nature, who should concentrate in a particular point all the actions of a multitude of men, and should consider the laws from this point of view: maximum happiness divided among the greatest number of people. Happy are those few nations that passed good laws without waiting for either slow motion of chance or of human vicissitudes to take place. In this manner, they avoided having to pass laws generated by existing evil situations for the well-being of the population. And that philosopher . . . deserves the gratitude of mankind . . . for having planted the first seeds of useful truths.

In talking about the laws made by one generation of legislators and binding on the people of the future generations, Thomas Paine, in his *Rights of Man*, says that the "laws of every country must be analogous to some common principle." Then he expands on the argument:

Those who have quitted the world, and those who are not yet arrived at it, are as remote from each other as the utmost stretch of mortal imagination can conceive. What possible obligation, then, can exist between them; what rule or principle can be laid down that of two non-entities, the one out of existence and the other not in, and who can never meet in this world, the one should control the other to the end of time?

Lacking the eloquence and intensity of Paine, Beccaria, the cool examiner of human nature, had already treated the same argument. Yet, though lacking the intensity of Paine, Beccaria becomes more poignant, calling "iniquitous" such laws as come down through oaths:

. . . The judges have not received the laws from our ancient forefathers, as we receive a domestic tradition or a testament requesting posterity the care to obey; they receive the laws from living society or from the sovereign who represents it as the legitimate depositary composed of everyone's will. They do not receive them conditioned by obligations of an ancient oath — such oaths would be void if not iniquitous if they were to be received, because they would bind men of different epochs without the possibility of agreement . . .

The necessity of good laws for a government, in order to guarantee the rights of the very people forming that government, was uppermost in the minds of Paine and of Adams, and of the rest of the enlightened founders of this country's government. They believed, as Beccaria did, that good laws prevent criminal acts —"Crimes are acts of Tyranny of one or more on another or more." The laws also serve as a brake for those individuals bent on taking advantage of a people's temporary discontent in order to seize power and establish a despotic government worse than the one deposed, and utilizing the same men that helped in the seizure of the power. The citizens become the victims of themselves and serve as the means in maintaining another's tyranny.

In a country lacking good laws, the government leaves itself wide open to discontent and to its possible substitution. "Do you want to prevent crimes?" asks Beccaria, who considers the forceful overthrow of government a crime, then:

Be sure that wise men be the companions of liberty. The evils that arise from knowledge are in inverse ratio to their diffusion whereas the benefits are in direct ratio. A daring impostor who is never an ordinary individual, is always adored by the masses and scorned by the enlightened . . . [But] when in a nation the enlightened individuals are profusely dispersed throughout the land, the slanderous ignorance will be silenced, and the authority which is disarmed by reason will tremble, leaving immobile the vigorous force of the laws; because there is no enlightened individual that does not love the public, the clear, and the useful contracts of the

21

common security, especially when comparing that little bit of useless liberty sacrificed by him with the maximum of all the liberties sacrificed by other men, who without laws, could become his conspirators.

It may be a strange coincidence that in talking about "daring impostors" both John Adams and Thomas Paine should have used two figures from Italian history — men who, on taking advantage of the political crisis, and by duping the crowd, were able to overthrow the governments and assume power for themselves. But the very mob that made the seizure possible, on feeling a more despotic form of government from those individuals who had, among other things, promised liberty and given otherwise, on discovering the true nature of the impostors reacted with as much swiftness in murdering them as they did in destroying the legal but otherwise ineffective prior government.

In his *Common Sense*, Paine urges the colonists to proclaim a Charter with which to establish the independence of the colonies from England:

> A government of our own is our natural right: and when a man seriously reflects on the precariousness of human affairs, he will become convinced, that it is infinitely wiser and safer, to form a constitution of our own in a cool deliberate manner, while we have it in our power, than to trust such an interesting event to time and chance. If we omit it now, some Massanello may hereafter arise, who, laying hold of popular disquietudes, may collect together the desperate and the discontented, and by assuming to themselves the powers of government, finally sweep away the liberties of the Continent like a deluge.

(Thomas Aniello (1620-1647), otherwise known by his Neapolitan nickname of Masaniello, was the leader of the popular successful revolt of 1647 of the Neapolitans against the tyrannical government of the Spaniards. Immediately after the revolt, the people made him their captain. But soon Masaniello took advantage of his power and began to overstep his authority. When he reverted to cruelty in order to achieve his goals, those people who had made him their captain killed him in the same year he had gotten into power).

John Adams, writing his Diary in the summer of 1797, reflected on another character of Italian history, the Roman, Cola di Rienzo (1314-1354), a forerunner of the late Duce. Cola envisioned a second Roman Empire with Rome at its center. In attempting to fulfill his dreams, he organized the various free communes of Italy in opposition to the nobility and to the church, whose Pope was living in a type of exile in Avignon. Having been defeated by the latter, Cola was exiled to Prague. Upon his release, he returned to Rome as a free man. Once again, he organized the people and succeeded in establishing a new government for the city of Rome. At first, the people fought for him and assured him the throne. But soon, he became infatuated with his power and began to abuse the very people that had empowered him. The people revolted and amassed beneath his palace. Cola, shrewd as he was unpredictable, dressed in disguise and secretly made his way into the heart of the mob, shouting with them, "Down with Cola; kill Cola." Then, the story goes, something went wrong with the disguise and he was recognized. Thereupon and without hesitation, the crowd turned on him and killed him right on the spot.

Reflecting on Cola, John Adams is reminiscent of Beccaria's observations in attempting to answer why these incidents take place. In his opinion, such incidents are generated by defective and outdated laws, which in turn give way to despotism.

It must be accepted that in the minds of the founders of this country's government, the concern of wanting to avert such despotism must have been of tantamount importance. It cannot be a pure coincidence that in the many years over which the U. S. government has been in force, it has not had any such usurpation; and it must have been due to the safeguards incorporated within the various documents against possibilities of a Masaniello or of a Cola, or, for that matter, against a French Revolution's Robespierre.

It is interesting to note Adams' observations over both Petrarca and Cola, as he writes in his Diary of 31 July 1796:

> . . . Reading the second Volume of Petrarch's Life. This singular character had very wild Notions of the Right of the City of Rome to a Republican Government and the Empire of the World. It is strange that his Infatuation for Rienzi did not expose him to more Resentment and greater Danger. In the Absence of the Pope at Avignon, and the People having no regular Check upon the Nobles, these fell into their usual Dissentions, and oppressed the People till they were ripe to be duped by any single Enthusiast, bold Adventurer, ambitious Usurper, or hypocritical Villain who should, with sufficient Imprudence, promise them justice, (Humanity), Clemency, and Liberty.

Confronted with a vast land area over which to govern, the early Americans like Adams, Washington, and Jefferson surely must have thought about the problem of governing such an area without turning to despotism. Beccaria had considered the question, saying that "a too vast republic cannot save itself from despotism unless it subdivides itself into so many little federal republics."

Yet when the time came to ratify the Constitution which was to govern the federated states, the question came up concerning the introductory remark — should it be, "We, the States," or, "We, the people"?

Regardless of how many smaller republics a nation may divide itself into, according to Beccaria, it always has to be a "union of people," all counted as individual citizens. When, on the other hand, a society or a nation is based on units such as states or families, and not on the single members as units of that union, then we have a union of families or of states and not a union of men.

"If there are one hundred thousand men," observes Beccaria, "or rather twenty thousand families each consisting of five members including the head who represents the family, and the association of the society is made of families, then there would be twenty thousand men and eighty thousand slaves. But if the association is composed of men, there would be one hundred thousand citizens and no slaves. In the first case there would be a republic together with twenty thousand little monarchies; in the second instance, the republican spirit will breathe not only in the public squares and in the nation's assemblies, but in each home as well where the greater part of men's happiness and misery is to be found."

To what extent, then, this thought served to retain the phrasing, "We, the people," cannot be completely known. But that the Constitution was supposed to be the supreme law of the land has certainly come to fruition. It is this kind of law, a law that aims at the single individual rather than at units, that Beccaria was principally concerned with — it being the means to regulate the activities of men and to assure them their happiness on earth.

To continue to insist that Beccaria was influential only with the reforms of criminal law does injustice to him as a man and as a philosopher.

In the case of Europe, he had tremendous impact because there was need to reform the criminal laws. But in America, the need was to secure laws that would guarantee a form of government of the people, by the people, and for the people; and Beccaria's book, if it was at all influential, was so in this respect: not having had the right to reform laws, our forefathers created them — and Beccaria was influential in the shaping of the basic code of American laws.

"When the republic is made up of men, the family does not become subordinate to command, but becomes subordinate to contract instead; and the children, when they are of the age when they are free from dependence on nature — which con-

25

Montville Twp Public Library 9504469

sists of that weakness and need of education and of self-protection — then they become free members of the city, and become subjects of their own free will to the head of the family in partaking of the advantages as do the free men of a great society. In the first case, the children — which form the greater part and the most useful to the nation — are at the discretion of the father; in the second case, there exists but one tie of command, which is that sacred and inviolable tie of administering reciprocally the necessary succor, and that of gratitude for the received benefits, which gratitude is not so much destroyed by the malice of the human heart as by a misunderstood subjection by the laws." It might be added at this point that in the society of Beccaria, there are no nobles by birthright, for the system of the nobility automatically and historically forms family units and breathes a caste system that benefits the few at the expense of the many.

In her book, *Jefferson the Road to Glory* 1743-1776, Marie Kimball insists on the traditional concept of Beccaria's role as the one responsible for the reform of criminal laws. She proves her point through Jefferson, who without doubt admired Beccaria's book.

"Revision of the laws concerning crimes and punishments lay in Jefferson's particular sphere as a revisor," she says; then states that Jefferson had "no less than twenty-six extracts from Beccaria," and that Jefferson "absorbed Beccaria's ideas, along with those of many other writers, by the time he started to prepare his 'Bill for proportioning crimes and punishments in cases heretofore capital.'"

While these observations are true, to limit oneself to parroting the same remarks is to limit the thrust of Beccaria's book, especially in connection with individuals of the calibre of Jefferson, the man and the driving force behind the creation, and not the reformation or the revision, of the body of laws that were to be accepted as "The King."

Were the scope of Beccaria to be limited to crime and punishment, as purported by the title, the book should contain an abundance of words such as "crime" and "punishment." The fact is that Beccaria frequently, if not compulsorily, used such words as "law," "liberty," "rights," "justice," "republic," "human being," "poor wretch," "tyranny," "happiness," — the conclusion being that where there are good laws the people enjoy the attributes of happiness; whereas, where there are bad laws, the people are subjected to the attributes of tyranny.

Vittorio Alfieri, a contemporary of Beccaria, has perhaps given the best definition of tyranny: "Any government whatever in which those having the responsibility for the execution of the laws become tyrants when they make or destroy them, break them, interpret them, impede them, or even only delude with the security of impunity."

A tyrant utilizes the laws as he sees fit; the laws become his tool. It is exactly this that Beccaria wants to avoid, and it is exactly this type of tyranny that men such as Jefferson, Adams, and Paine wanted to destroy.

In the Declaration of Independence, the intention is expressed much as Beccaria might have wished:

When in the Course of human Events, it becomes necessary for one People to dissolve the Political Bands which have connected them with another, and to assume among the Powers of the Earth, the separate and equal Station to which the Laws of Nature's God entitle them, a decent Respect to the Opinions of Mankind requires that they should declare the causes which impel them to the Separation.

After this very eloquent and sustained introduction, wherein equality of mankind is defined within the limits of the laws, the Representatives of the future United States of America assembled in General Congress on 4 July 1776 to spell out their past history in connection with the tyranny of the English King, as follows:

"The History of the present King of Great Britain is a History of repeated Injuries and Usurpations, all having in direct Object the Establishment of an absolute Tyranny over these States. To prove this, let Facts be submitted to a candid World."

(Of the twenty-seven "Facts," the first four are very significant):

"He has refused his Assent to Laws, the most wholesome and necessary for the Public Good."

"He has forbidden his Governors to pass Laws of immediate and pressing Importance, unless suspended in their Operation till his Assent should be obtained; and when so suspended, he has utterly neglected to attend them."

"He has refused to pass other Laws for the Accomodation of large Districts of People, unless those People could relinquish the Right of Representation in the Legislature, a Right inestimable to them and formidable to Tyrants only."

"He has called together Legislative Bodies at Places unusual, uncomfortable, and distant from the Depository of their public Records, for the sole Purpose of fatiguing them into Compliance with his Measures."

In view of all those abuses, it is no wonder that the fifty-seven men, twenty of whom were lawyers, should conclude to support the Declaration of Independence by pledging to each other "their lives, their fortunes, and their sacred honor"; for, in the conditions under which they were living, their lives, their fortune, and their honor had no meaning.

One of the young men to sign the document was the thirty-three-year-old lawyer-farmer from Virginia — Jefferson, and the forty-year-old lawyer from Massachusetts — John Adams. These two men are singled out for the role they played in stating the conditions under which they were living in the colonies. What was now needed was another document incorporating safeguards against the very things they were suffering.

With the Constitution of 1787, we see transcribed the ideals of the Declaration of Independence into a document having the scope to establish procedure through which to form and run the new government. Remarkable is the clarity of the language which aims at the essence of things rather than on their details — and this is perhaps why the document is still guiding a nation that has seen a geometric growth in territory and in population since the memorable year of 1787.

In his chapter on crime prevention, Beccaria speaks of laws in general. His observations, however, are applicable across the board; and the implications, for sure, reach beyond the field of criminal law:

"Do you want to prevent crimes?" Beccaria asks. "Then, be sure that the laws are clear and simple, and that the whole strength of the nation be condensed in order to defend them and that no part of that strength be employed to destroy them. Make sure that the laws favor less the various classes of men and more and more the individual men themselves."

The language of Beccaria and that of his American contemporaries is as clear as it is concise in establishing that whatever is done be done for the people, and that the strength of the nation be utilized to defend rather than to destroy the laws, remembering that good laws are those reflecting the needs of the living people.

The rights of the people are further strengthened in the first ten amendments to the Constitution, known as the Bill of Rights.

In his book, *A History of Italian Literature,* Ernest Hatch Wilkins, one of the first of American scholars to point out the importance of Beccaria to early American thought, speaks about Beccaria's book:

"The treatise was immediately and very widely influential. It was translated into a score of languages, and led to the revisions of several penal codes. The first English translation appeared in 1767; a reprint of that translation issued in New York in 1773 is, with a single unimportant exception, the first translation of an Italian work to be published in this country. The influence of Beccaria's thought is manifest in the American Bill of Rights."

The very first right of the Bill of Rights is perhaps the most far-reaching in that it prohibits Congress from passing any law that might respect "an establishment of religion, or prohibiting the free exercise thereof."

What turns out to be separation of church and state, and, in any event, the freedom of the citizens to practice whatever form of religion they wish both on an individual or collective level, is an extension of Beccaria's desire as expressed in the chapter on a "particular kind of crime." Without mentioning the crimes committed under the name of religion, Beccaria nevertheless makes us understand what the early Americans understood well enough to put into practice, that while all other nations have had religious strifes of the types seen as recently as the 1970 decade in Ireland and between Pakistan and India, the United States of America, with the exception of local incidents, has not undergone the frightening crimes related to religious activities. Without a doubt, this is due to the far-sightedness of those who wrote the First Amendment.

The modern Americans who consider the perfunctory recital of empty prayer words in public places may well consider Beccaria's worries:

> Reasonable men will see that the place, the century, and the subject matter do not permit me to examine the nature of such crimes. It would take me too long and far wide from my subject matter in order to prove how . . . opinions which differ from each other only by some very subtle and obscure variances, altogether beyond human capability to understand, how they can still upset the public welfare when one opinion is not authorized in preference over the others.

Yet nowhere does Beccaria make any statement against the practice of religion either by an individual or by a group. On the other hand, Beccaria upholds the right of freedom of religion, which freedom ceases to exist as soon as, by act of law, any part of any religion becomes the official representative of any arm of a given government.

"The principle of Beccaria is sound," says Jefferson, contemplating the laws that gave the clergy special privileges. Yet, there is no need to have any type of pardons specified by either the law or by the Executive, for, "when laws are made as mild as they should be, both those pardons are absurd. The principle of Beccaria is sound. Let the legislators be merciful, but the executors of the law inexorable." The clergy have to be as responsible to the laws as are any other citizens; and, as no one can receive special privileges by the laws themselves, religion — no matter how neutral (neutrality is impossible in religion) — must not be officially recognized by any part of a constituted government.

The belief that a little bit of religion cannot do harm especially among the young, and in the morning before classes, is a view held by many well-intentioned people, not realizing that habit, as observed by Beccaria, is often the worst of the tyrants. And, the very fact that in twentieth century America, prayer has become an issue due to the complaints by those who do not believe in the message of the supposedly very neutral prayer (as though prayers can be neutral), should be enough to convince the proponents of prayer in public places that men such as Jefferson, Adams, and Beccaria must have seen the harm and danger brought about by such innocuous practices and concluded that the best way to avert strife was to allow religions to be practiced freely and on an individual basis.

We can reiterate Beccaria's observation on what happens when one opinion is authorized over another; how, as a result, this preference can upset the public welfare, and even bring about revolts and wars.

In conclusion, it seems very fair to say that Beccaria's role on the European scene was that of a reformer. The fact that so many codes were changed either directly or indirectly as a result of his book surely made him the reformer. This was possible because there were bad law codes to be reformed or revised. But in America, where the early Americans depended upon someone else's laws, there were no laws as such to reform or revise. They had the choice of obeying or not obeying. When they discovered that the English king was practicing his tyranny on them through English-made laws, the early Americans rebelled.

"He has refused his Assent to Laws, the most wholesome and necessary for the Public Good," was the first fact they enumerated against the king. Their goal, therefore, was not to reform — a right they did not have — but to reject in order to create, knowing all the while the risk of losing their lives, let alone their fortunes and honor. Fate wanted, however, that they should succeed in achieving their independence, and thereby set the stage in initiating the last phase of a historical cycle.

Beccaria's role in this process, must have been to serve as a source of engendering that spirit of humanity reflected in those early American documents.

It is a well known fact that Jefferson, in his draft of the Declaration of Independence, first wrote "life, liberty, and property," and then changed it to "life, liberty, and the pursuit of happiness." May not this revision have been due to the influence of Beccaria's thought?

Chapter 2.

BECCARIA: HIS LIFE AND TIMES

The life of Beccaria, as a young eighteenth-century noble-man, was hardly predictable as an influence on the revolutionary epoch then germinating. Marquis Cesare Bonesana di Beccaria was born of an aristocratic family on 15 March 1738 in Milan, Italy, where he also died in 1794. As a child, he was educated by the Jesuists of Parma. In 1758, he received his law degree from the University of Pavia, dissatisfied, however, with the type of education he had received. Against his father's wishes, Beccaria married a certain Teresa Blasco in February 1761, breaking his relations with his father, and quickly finding himself in poverty.

At the age of twenty-two, he began to read the authors of the Enlightenment, especially Montesquieu, whose *Lettres Persanes* made possible his intellectual conversion. This conversion must have been reinforced through his participation in the challenging discussions held by a group of friends belonging to the academy of "Pugni," who no doubt contributed inspiration, if not collaboration, to his achievement.

At the time of Beccaria, there were many such groups in Italy, often going under the names of academies. Among the more important ones, this Academia dei Pugni was founded by Pietro Verri in 1760. The members of this group, proposing to deal with various cultural aspects of the period as promulgators and educators of the new culture, published their thoughts in their literary magazine, "Caffè," appearing in Brescia every ten days. Beccaria became one of their more important members. The others were the Verri brothers, and Frisi, Bitti, Lambertenghi, Visconti, Longo, and others. With the exception of Beccaria, above all, and of the Verri brothers, none of the original members achieved any fame.

The other two academies were that of the "Granelleschi" which was founded in Venice by the Gozzi brothers, and that of the "Trasformati" of which the poet Parini was a member. The three vied to do several things and were often at odds with each other. That of the "Pugni," for instance, wished to introduce foreign elements into what they considered a stifled Italian culture; that of the "Granelleschi" wished to retain the purity of the Italian culture and fought against the introduction of foreign elements; and that of the "Trasformati" maintained a middle-of-the-road policy. Among the better known men of this time were Parini, who published his very famous didactic-satirical poem, *Il Giorno* (The Day), begun in 1760; Alfieri with his tragedies and his two formidable political essays, *Della Tirannide* (On Tyranny), 1777, and *Del Principe e delle lettere* (The Prince and the Men of Letters) 1786; and Giuseppe Baretti with his magazine, "Frusta letteraria" (Literary Whip), founded in 1763, through which he attempted to rejuvenate Italian culture.

Beccaria participated in this challenging period of transition that later was to bring forth men of the calibre of Ugo Foscolo, Giacomo Leopardi, and Alessandro Manzoni. In any event, Beccaria's literary production remained rather meager, due mainly to his laziness. In all, he left us only five articles of various interest, and four essays: *Del disordine e dei rimedi delle monete nello Stato di Milano nell'ano* 1762, published in Lucca in 1762; his celebrated *Dei delitti e delle pene*, published in Livorno (Leghorn) in 1764; his *Elementi di economia publica*, published posthumously in Milano in 1804; and his *Ricerche intorno alla natura dello stile*, published in 1770. Aside from his work on criminal law which received world-wide acclaim, the others had little impact on the general public.

It is doubtful that Beccaria would have written his book had it not been for the suggestion given him by his friends of the academy. They proposed to him to treat the subject of the state of criminal law as it was practiced throughout Europe, and he luckily accepted.

34

Immediately upon publication, his book received wide acclaim and the usual severe criticism. With the translation of Morellet, the book appeared in France, where it received a rather cool reception at first as witnessed by the somewhat indifferent appraisal of D'Alembert; however, upon reading the second edition, the French philosopher suddenly became an admirer of the work, along with Diderot and Voltaire (both of whom wrote commentaries on the book), and, Holbach, Helvetius, Buffon, Thomas, Hume, and even Hegel.

It is generally agreed that the tremendous success must have been due to the manner in which Beccaria brought into focus the subject of the deplorable state of crime and punishment in relation to criminal laws and procedures. The effect was so immediate that even Catherine II of Russia invited Beccaria to go to Petersburg, along with Voltaire and other men of the Enlightenment. But the Italian officials who were under Austrian rule at this time created a Chair for Beccaria in Milan, thus compelling him to remain in his country. While in his Chair, as professor in economics, in his lectures he anticipated the economic theories of Adam Smith and the theories of Thomas Robert Malthus on population and subsistence.

He left Italy, however, to visit Paris — a trip he could not refuse due to the clamorous and persistent invitation from the residents of the universally accepted cultural capital of the world. He made the journey to Paris, together with his friend Pietro Verri. But the fanfare and the tremendous attention directed toward him was too much for him. Because of his inability to capitalize on his fame, Beccaria decided to return to Italy, leaving his friend Verri to continue with the celebration — it is said that Beccaria was anxious to get back to Italy so that he could be with his newly married wife, a young woman by the name of Anna from the family of Count Barnaba of Barbo.

On 29 April 1771, Beccaria was elected a member of the Supreme Council of the economy. He was active more or less in this capacity until 1791 when he was made a member of the official group whose goal was to reform the civil and criminal judicial system of Italy. He died 28 November 1794.

Cesare Beccaria lived during the time of the Enlightenment, and that of the American Revolution and later of the abortive French Revolution. Like most of the intellectuals of the time, he came under the sway of the Cartesian philosophy which upheld the supremacy of the rational over the sensitive individual. Yet, though he was to receive the main stimulus for his work from Montesquieu's *Lettres persanes,* and from Rousseau's *Contract Social,* asserted that society is composed of individuals willing to give up part of their liberty — the least possible — in order to achieve a common utility for all. Beccaria describes it this way:

> Laws are the conditions with which independent and isolated men united into society, being tired of having lived in a continuous state of war and of having enjoyed a liberty made useless by the uncertainty of not being able to conserve it. They sacrificed part of their liberty in order to enjoy what was left of it in security and tranquility. The sum total of these portions of liberty sacrificed to the welfare of each man, form the sovereignty of a nation whose ruler is the legitimate depository and administrator . . .
>
> Necessity, therefore, compelled men to give up a portion of individual liberty; it is certain therefore that each man does not want to place in the public depository but the least portion possible, just enough to compel others to defend him.

What may be unusual is the fact that Beccaria amplified an observation made by Rousseau. But what may turn out to be more unusual is the possibility that Beccaria may have been affected by the Vichian philosophy of Gianbattista Vico rather than by that of the enlightened encyclopedists whose source, without a doubt, was Cartesian.

The Encyclopedists, for example, would never say, in attempting to solve a human problem, "Let us look into our hearts for an answer " they would turn to the rational mind which they made the depository and source of all human activities. Beccaria, on the other hand, said that whatever is based on the sentiment of man is apt to be good:

> From political morality we cannot hope for any lasting advantages unless it is founded on indelible sentiments of man. Whatever law that should deviate from these sentiments will always encounter with a contrary resistance which in the end will always win out, just as a small force evenly distributed will eventually win over any violent motion exerted to a mass.

Beccaria refers to the "sentiments of man," a phrase that would be practically absent from the vocabulary of the men of the Enlightenment — naturally, this is meant only from the point of view that sentiment is placed in opposition to the pure mind or thought process. The first to contradict this principle may have been Vico in his *New Science* published in 1725, wherein he affirms that *"Nihil est in intellectu quin prius fuerit in sensu."*

Vico further took the following position with respect to intellect, to reflection, and to philosophical logic. He placed fantasy against intellect, intuition against reflection, and poetic logic against philosophical logic. In other words, Vico reasserts man's sentiments as being at the base of all present and future experience. How man "feels" and what he "feels," therefore, may disclose a superior sense of justice than might be gotten from a purely intellectualized process.

From this may follow that, in Beccaria, justice in brought down to human level; or better still, justice is brought down to the "sensitive" level through which man is humanized. The principles, then, through which man is to be punished, should he transgress, are to be found in our hearts.

"Let us consult the human heart," says Beccaria, for, "in it, we will find the fundamental principles of the sovereign's true rights to punish crimes."

Beccaria is confident of man's sensibility. He places more faith on the role of man's heart in solving the more crucial problems involving man's relations to other men than on men's intellect, which too often leads astray — but does not say that the opposite is not also true. In this respect, Beccaria goes counter to that whole movement that finally was to culminate in the French Revolution.

The roots to Beccaria's philosophy must reside in Vico's historiography where Vico speaks of the courses and re-courses of history, dividing the cycle of history as revolving around three basic stages that keep on repeating themselves more or less consistently — the three stages being that of the Gods or the supernatural, that of the Heroes of the type of Achilles, and that of Man. The latter stage would deal with those relationships which, in their application, limit the roles of the supernatural and of the heroic, and emphasize the role of men in their social interaction with the overall goal of achieving maximum happiness for the largest number of people.

It is to be asked, then, to what extent Beccaria bases himself on Vico, especially when Beccaria approaches his subject matter in much the same manner as Vico: "Moral and politcal principles which regulate mankind come from three sources: revelation, natural law, and man-made conventions," says Beccaria, who then goes on to discuss the various relationships among the three. (Vico had spoken of the three stages: that of the supernatural, that of the hereos, and that of man).

Gianbattista Vico was very little known and accepted during his lifetime; his writings were even less understood. As a result, he came to be known as the obscure philosopher who did nothing more than amass thousands of details indiscriminately put down in forms incomprehensible to his contemporaries. The problem was not Vico's, however; but it must have centered around the manner in which he proceeded with his exposition. He moved in single units which he called "degnità" — basic units of truth he discovered as governing the universe with all that is in it. These basic units of truth, also known as axioms, may be the ones that Beccaria refers to when contemplating the role of legislation through which mankind is to secure its happiness:

. . . that philosopher deserves the gratitude of mankind for having had the courage (from his detested and obscure study) of planting among the people the first seeds — for so long unharvested — of the useful truths.

That Beccaria's "philosopher" may be Vico has not been suggested. Yet it is difficult to discard altogether the possibility of an allusion to Vico. Likewise, it is difficult to reject altogether the possibility that Thomas Paine may also have had some knowledge of Vico's historiography, especially when, in his *Rights of Man*, he states a Vichian observation: "First was a Government of Priestcraft, the second of Conquerors, and the third of Reason."

If with his "that Philosopher," Baccaria refers to Vico, then we can say that those "first seeds . . . of useful truths" did not go unharvested for too long a time, considering that the book *On Crimes and Punishments* may possibly be the first fruit to mature and to be harvested.* It can also be added without fear that the useful truths uncovered in Beccaria's book have been incorporated in practically all of the constitutions of the countries of Europe. The same truths which matured in that little book also reached the new continent, penetrating into those lofty spirits who said:

We hold these Truths to be self-evident, that all Men are created equal, that they are endowed by their Creator with certain unalienable Rights, that among these are Life, Liberty, and the Pursuit of Happiness — That to secure these Rights, Governments are instituted among Men, deriving their just Powers from the Consent of the Governed, that whenever any Form of Government becomes destructive of these Ends, it is the Right of the People to alter or to abolish it, and to institute new Gov-

39

ernment, laying its Foundation on such Principles, and organizing its Powers in such Form, as to them shall seem most likely to effect their Safety and happiness.

And thus, we have the very first document that may have initiated the third phase or stage of Vico's historiography wherein Man comes into being.

---

*Here is an example as expressed in *Degnita* VII: Legislation considers man what he is, in order to assign him those tasks that are amenable to his capabilities, for the good of the society; in the manner in which brutality, avarice, and ambition can bring humanity to its perdition, the soldier, the merchant, and the court, on the other hand, can bring strength, opulence, and knowledge to the republic. The three vices would certainly destroy mankind and preclude man from achieving the desired civil happiness.

This axiom proves that there exists divine Providence, and that there is a divine legislative mind which has made possible for men to live in a human society through civil order, who otherwise would live as beasts in the wilderness, because every man is guided by the passion to seek out his own interests first.

Chapter 3

EARLY EDITIONS AND TRANSLATIONS OF BECCARIA'S ON CRIMES AND PUNISHMENTS

The first edition of *Dei delitti e delle pene* appeared in Livorno, Italy, in July 1764, printed and published by a certain Coltellini of Livorno. At the time of publication, Beccaria was twenty-six years old.

A second edition, revised and corrected, appeared during the same year in Monaco. This edition had 112 pages — eight more than the first edition.

The third edition appeared the following year in Lausanne. This edition contained 229 pages. The additional pages were due to the various answers Beccaria wrote in response to criticism and to charges that were published against his book and against him as a person. This edition also included the first additions on the part of the author to the basic text. The book, however, found its way into the listing of the Roman Index through the efforts of the preacher Fachinei.

In 1766 there appeared two editions in Harlem; in 1767, another edition in Buglion, France. Subsequently there appeared in Dublin another edition with an English translation and a commentary attributed to M. de Voltaire; this edition was published in Dublin but printed by J. Exshaw. A similar edition appeared in London the same year. Another edition appeared in London in 1769 and one in 1770 together with another in Glasgow.

In America, the first edition in translation supposedly appeared in print in 1773, as it was advertised as "in press" by the Rivington, New York, *Gazetter* on 28 October 1773. As yet, a copy of this edition has not been found. The earliest edition of which there are still some copies, appeared in Philadelphia in

1776, and includes the commentary attributed to Voltaire. In 1777, another edition appeared in Charlestown, South Carolina; it was printed and sold by David Bruce, at his shop in Charles Street. The title page indicates that the commentary is attributed to Voltaire; it does not show Beccaria as the author, however. In 1778, another edition appeared in Philadelphia, printed and sold by R. Bell, next door to St. Paul's Church, on Third Street. Ten years later, another edition appeared in South Carolina. Meanwhile, editions had appeared in Dublin, London, Glasgow, etc. Several editions appeared in Edinburg alone. During this time, the book appeared in translation in practically every cultural center of Europe and America.

It may be added as an item of curiosity that the first of Voltaire's works published in America was his *The Man Worth Forty Crowns*, appearing in Philadelphia in 1778. In the same year, his *Miscellanies* appeared, and in 1796 came out his *Philosophical Dictionary*. Rousseau's *Confessions*, on the other hand, was first published in America in 1796. The *Spirit of the Law* of Montesquieu — Beccaria's idol in more ways than one — was first published in America in 1802. It might also be added that, according to *The National Union Catalog Pre-1956 Imprints*, William Young, in his "A new edition corrected," erroneously lists the edition as having been published in 1763, and Beccaria born in 1735.

In the twentieth century, Beccaria's book continues to be translated. In 1963, H. Paolucci made a translation which was published by Bobbs-Merrill. The following year, K. Foster and J. Grigson translated it in England, publishing it under the title of *The Column of Infamy*, a work written by Beccaria's grandson, Alessandro Manzoni. Beccaria's works have recently been published by Sansoni of Florence. The two volumes edited by Sergio Romagnoli contain all of Beccaria's works, including his poetry and essay on Style, as well as Romagnoli's ample introduction and bibliographical notes.

Nowhere in the two volumes does Romagnoli mention either Adams or Jefferson, or the editions that appeared in the United States around the time of the Revolution. Other editions in translation are appearing in other parts of the world.

The reason for so many editions throughout the years might be due to one fact — the issues raised by Beccaria have not yet been resolved; and many scholars together with many humanitarian reformers may feel that in Beccaria we may still find the inspiration if not the solutions to some of our grave problems such as Capital Punishment, Secret Accusations, Gun Control, Public Prayer, Crime Prevention, Law Reforms, Abortion, and others.

AN
ESSAY
ON
CRIMES
AND
PUNISHMENTS

Tranflated from the ITALIAN;

WITH A
COMMENTARY,

Attributed to Monf. DE VOLTAIRE.

Tranflated from the FRENCH.

In rebus quibufcumque difficilioribus non expecta ..m, ut quis
fimul, & ferat, & metat, fed præparatione opus eft, ut per gradus
..aturefcant.   BACON.

STATE OF SOUTHCAROLINA.

PRINTED AND SOLD BY DAVID BRUCE, AT
HIS SHOP IN CHURCH-STREET, CHARLESTOWN,
M DCC LXXVII.

AN
ESSAY
ON
CRIMES
AND
PUNISHMENTS.

WRITTEN BY THE

MARQUIS BECCARIA,

OF MILAN.

WITH A
COMMENTARY,

Attributed to Monfieur De VOLTAIRE.

In the prefent age, we feem univerfally aiming at perfection;
let us not therefore forget to perfect the LAWS, on which
our LIVES and FORTUNES depend.   *Voltaire.*

Wherever truth and intereft fhall embrace,
Let paffion cool, and prejudice give place.   *Brooke.*

PHILADELPHIA:

Printed and Sold by R. BELL, next Door to St. Paul's
Church, in Third-Street.

M. DCC. LXXVIII.

Iohn Adams.

ADAMS 151.13

Thomas B Adams. From his Father
1800

A N

E S S A Y

O N

C R I M E S

A N D

P U N I S H M E N T S,

TRANSLATED FROM THE ITALIAN;

W I T H A

C O M M E N T A R Y,

ATTRIBUTED TO

Monf. De V O L T A I R E,

TRANSLATED FROM THE FRENCH.

***

THE FOURTH EDITION.

In rebus quibufcumque difficilioribus non expectandum,
ut quis fimul, & ferat, & metat, fed præparatione opus
eft, ut per gradus maturefcant.

BACON.

***

LONDON:

Printed for F. NEWBERY, at the Corner of
St. Paul's Church-Yard.

M DCC LXXV.

PREFACE

OF THE

TRANSLATOR

TO THE FIRST EDITION.

PENAL LAWS, so consider-
able a part of every system of
legislation, and of so great importance to the happiness, peace, and
security of every member of society,
are still so imperfect, and are attended with so many unnecessary
circumstances of cruelty in all nations, that an attempt to reduce
them to the standard of reason must

A 2   be

be interefting to all mankind.   It
is not furprifing, then, that this little book hath engaged the attention
of all ranks of people in every part
of Europe.   It is now about eighteen
months fince the firft publication;
in which time it hath paffed no lefs
than fix editions in the original language;   the third of which was
printed within fix months after its
firft appearance.   It hath been tranflated into French; that tranflation
hath alfo been feveral times reprinted, and perhaps no book, on any
fubject, was ever received with more
avidity, more generally read, or
more univerfally applauded.

THE author is the *Marquis* BEC-
CARIA, of *Milan.*   Upon confidering the nature of the religion and
govern-

government under which he lives, the reasons for concealing his name are obvious; the whole was read, at different times, in a society of learned men in that city, and was published at their desire. As to the translation, I have preserved the order of the original, except in a paragraph or two, which I have taken the liberty to restore to the chapters to which they evidently belong, and from which they must have been accidentally detached. The French translator hath gone much farther; he hath not only transposed every chapter, but every paragraph in the whole book. But in this, I conceive, he hath assumed a right which belongs not to any translator, and which cannot be justified. His disposition may appear more systematical,

A 3

atical, but certainly the author hath as undoubted a right to the arrangement of his own ideas, as to the ideas themselves ; and therefore, to deſtroy that arrangement, is to pervert his meaning, if he had any meaning in his plan, the contrary to which can hardly be ſuppoſed.

WITH regard to the commentary, attributed to Monſ. de Voltaire, my only authority for ſuppoſing it his, is the voice of the public, which indeed is the only authority we have for moſt of his works. Let thoſe who are acquainted with the peculiarity of his manner judge for themſelves.

THE facts above-mentioned would preclude all apology for this tranſla-
tion,

tion, if any apology were neceffary, for tranflating into our language, a work which, from the nature of the fubject, muft be interefting to every nation; but muft be
particularly acceptable to the Eng-
lifh, from the eloquent and forcible
manner in which the author pleads
the caufe of liberty, benevolence
and humanity. It may however
be objected, that a treatife of this
kind is ufelefs in England, where,
from the excellence of our laws
and government, no examples of
cruelty or oppreffion are to be
found. But it muft alfo be allowed,
that much is ftill wanting to perfect our fyftem of legiflation: the
confinement of debtors, the filth
and horror of our prifons, the cruelty

elty of jailors, and the extortion of the petty officers of justice, to all which may be added the melancholy reflection, that the number of criminals put to death in England is much greater than in any other part of Europe, are considerations which will sufficiently answer every objection. These are my only reasons for endeavouring to diffuse the knowledge of the useful truths contained in this little essay; and I say, with my author, that if I can be instrumental in rescuing a single victim from the hands of tyranny or ignorance, his transports will sufficiently console me for the contempt of all mankind.

T A B L E

O F

C O N T E N T S.

CONTENTS.

CONTENTS.

A COMMENTARY on the Book of CRIMES and PUNISHMENTS.

CONTENTS.

INTRODUCTION.

IN every human fociety, there is an effort continually tending to confer on one part the height of power and happinefs, and to reduce the other to the extreme of weaknefs and mifery. The intent of good laws is to oppofe this effort, and to diffufe their influence univerfally, and equally. But men generally abandon the care of their moft important concerns to the uncertain prudence and difcretion of thofe, whofe intereft it is to rejeČt the beft, and wifeft inftitutions; and it is not till they have been led into a thoufand miftakes in matters, the moft effential to their lives and liberties, and are weary of fuffering, that they can be induced to apply a remedy to the evils, with which they are oppreffed. It is then they begin to conceive, and acknowledge the moft palpable truths, which, from their very fimplicity, commonly efcape vulgar minds, incapable

B of

of analyfing objects, accuftomed to receive impreffions without diftinction, and to be determined rather by the opinions of others, than by the refult of their own examination.

If we look into hiftory we fhall find, that laws, which are, or ought to be, conventions between men in a ftate of freedom, have been, for the moft part, the work of the paffions of a few, or the confequences of a fortuitous, or temporary neceffity; not dictated by a cool examiner of human nature, who knew how to collect in one point, the actions of a multitude, and had this only end in view, *the greateft happinefs of the greateft number*. Happy are thofe few nations, who have not waited, till the flow fucceffion of human viciffitudes, fhould, from the extremity of evil, produce a tranfition to good; but, by prudent laws, have facilitated the progrefs from one to the other!⁹ And how great are the obligations due from mankind to that philofopher, who from the obfcurity of his clofet, had the courage to fcatter

amongft

amongſt the multitude, the ſeeds of uſeful truths, ſo long unfruitful!

THE art of printing has diffuſed the knowledge of thoſe philoſophical truths, by which the relations between ſovereigns and their ſubjects, and between nations, are diſcovered. By this knowledge, commerce is animated, and there has ſprung up a ſpirit of emulation, and induſtry, worthy of rational beings. Theſe are the produce of this enlightened age; but the cruelty of puniſhments, and the irregularity of proceeding in criminal caſes, ſo principal a part of the legiſlation, and ſo much neglected throughout Europe, has hardly ever been called in queſtion. Errors, accumulated through many centuries, have never yet been expoſed by aſcending to general principles; nor has the force of acknowledged truths been ever oppoſed to the unbounded licentiouſneſs of ill-directed power, which has continually produced ſo many authorized examples of the moſt unfeeling barbarity. Surely, the groans of the weak, ſacrificed to the cruel ignorance, and indo-

lence

lence of the powerful; the barbarous torments lavifhed, and multiplied with ufelefs
feverity, for crimes either not proved, or
in their nature impoffible; the filth and
horrors of a prifon, increafed by the moft
cruel tormentor of the miferable, uncertainty, ought to have roufed the attention
of thofe whofe bufinefs is to direct the opinions of mankind.ᴵᴵ

THE immortal MONTESQUIEU has but
flightly touched on this fubject. Truth,
which is eternally the fame, has obliged
me to follow the fteps of that great man:
but the ftudious part of mankind, for
whom I write, will eafily diftinguifh the
fuperftructure from the foundation. I fhall
be happy, if with him, I can obtain the
fecret thanks of the obfcure, and peaceful
difciples of reafon, and philofophy; and
excite that tender emotion, in which fenfible minds fympathize with him, who
pleads the caufe of humanity.

A N

E S S A Y

O N

CRIMES and PUNISHMENTS.

C H A P. I.

Of the Origin of Punishments.

LAWS are the conditions, under which men, naturally independent, united themselves in society. Weary of living in a continual state of war, and of enjoying a liberty which became of little value, from the uncertainty of its duration, they sacrificed one part of it, to enjoy the rest in

B 3   peace

peace and fecurity. The fum of all thefe portions of the liberty of each individual conftituted the fovereignty of a nation; and was depofited in the hands of the fovereign, as the lawful adminiftrator. But it was not fufficient only to eftablifh this depofite; it was alfo neceffary to defend it from the ufurpation of each individual, who will always endeavour to take away from the mafs, not only his own portion, but to encroach on that of others. Some motives, therefore, that ftrike the fenfes, were neceffary to prevent the defpotifm of each individual from plunging fociety into its former chaos. Such motives are the punifhments eftablifhed againft the infractors of the laws. I fay, that motives of this kind are neceffary; becaufe, experience fhews, that the multitude adopt no eftablifhed principle of conduct; and becaufe, fociety is prevented from approaching to that diffolution, (to which, as well as all other parts of the phyfical, and moral world, it naturally tends) only by motives, that are the immediate objects of fenfe, and which being continually prefented to the mind, are fuf-

ficient

ficient to counterbalance the effects of the passions of the individual, which oppose the general good. Neither the power of eloquence, nor the sublimest truths, are sufficient to restrain, for any length of time, those passions, which are excited by the lively impressions of present objects.

C H A P. II.

Of the Right to punish.

EVERY punishment, which does not arise from absolute necessity, says the great *Montesquieu*, is tyrannical. A proposition which may be made more general, thus. "Every act of authority of one man "over another, for which there is not an "absolute necessity, is tyrannical." It is upon this then, that the sovereign's right to punish crimes is founded; that is, upon the necessity of defending the public liberty, entrusted to his care, from the usurpation of individuals; and punishments are just in proportion, as the liberty, preserved by the sovereign, is sacred and valuable.

LET

LET us confult the human heart, and there we fhall find the foundation of the fovereign's right to punifh; for no advantage in moral policy can be lafting, which is not founded on the indelible fentiments of the heart of man. Whatever law deviates from this principle will always meet with a refiftance, which will deftroy it in the end; for the fmalleft force, continually applied, will overcome the moft violent motion communicated to bodies.

No man ever gave up his liberty, merely for the good of the public. Such a chimera exifts only in romances. Every individual wifhes, if poffible, to be exempt from the compacts, that bind the reft of mankind.

THE multiplication of mankind,[14] though flow, being too great for the means, which the earth, in its natural ftate, offered to fatisfy neceffities, which every day became more numerous, obliged men to feparate again, and form new focieties. Thefe naturally oppofed the firft, and a ftate of

war

war was transferred from individuals to
nations.

THUS it was neceffity that forced men
to give up a part of their liberty; it is
certain then, that every individual would
chufe to put into the public ftock the
fmalleft portion poffible; as much only as
was fufficient to engage others to defend
it.   The aggregate of thefe, the fmalleft
portions poffible, forms the right of punifhing: all that extends beyond this is
abufe, not juftice. [15]

OBSERVE, that by *juftice* I underftand
nothing more, than that bond, which is
neceffary to keep the intereft of individuals
united; without which, men would return
to their original ftate of barbarity. [16] All punifhments, which exceed the neceffity of
preferving this bond, are in their nature
unjuft.   We fhould be cautious how we
affociate with the word *juftice*, an idea of
any thing real, fuch as a phyfical power,
or a being that actually exifts.   I do not,
by any means, fpeak of the juftice of God,
which

which is of another kind, and refers immediately to rewards and punifhments in a
life to come.

C H A P. III.

Confequences of the foregoing Principles.

THE laws only can determine the punifhment of crimes; and the authority of making penal laws can only refide
with the legiflator, who reprefents the
whole fociety, united by the focial compact.
No magiftrate then (as he is one of the
fociety) can, with juftice, inflict on any
other member of the fame fociety, punifhment, that is not ordained by the laws.
But as a punifhment, increafed beyond the
degree fixed by the law, is the juft punifhment, with the addition of another; it
follows, that no magiftrate, even under a
pretence of zeal, or the public good, fhould
increafe the punifhment already determined
by the laws.

If

IF every individual be bound to fociety, fociety is equally bound to him, by a contract, which from its nature, equally binds both parties. This obligation, which defcends from the throne to the cottage, and equally binds the higheft, and loweft of mankind, fignifies nothing more, than that it is the intereft of all, that conventions, which are ufeful to the greateft number, fhould be punctually obferved. The violation of this compact by any individual, is an introduction to anarchy.

THE fovereign, who reprefents the fociety itfelf, can only make general laws, to bind the members; but it belongs not to him to judge whether any individual has violated the focial compact, or incurred the punifhment in confequence. For in this cafe, there are two parties, one reprefented by the fovereign, who infifts upon the violation of the contract, and the other is the perfon accufed, who denies it. It is neceffary then that there fhould be a third perfon to decide this conteft; that is to fay, a judge, or magiftrate, from whofe determination

mination there fhould be no appeal; and
this determination fhould confift of a fimple affirmation, or negation of fact. [18]

If it can only be proved, that the feverity of punifhments, though not immediately contrary to the public good, or to
the end for which they were intended, viz.
to prevent crimes, be ufelefs; then fuch
feverity would be contrary to thofe beneficent virtues, which are the confequence
of enlightened reafon, which inftructs the
fovereign to wifh rather to govern men in
a ftate of freedom and happinefs, than of
flavery. It would alfo be contrary to juftice, and the focial compact.

CHAP. IV.

Of the Interpretation of Laws.

JUDGES, in criminal cafes, have no
right to interpret the penal laws, becaufe they are not legiflators. They have
not received the laws from our anceftors as
a domeftic tradition, or as the will of a
teftator,

teſtator, which his heirs, and executors, are to obey; but they receive them from a ſociety actually exiſting, or from the ſovereign, its repreſentative. Even the authority of the laws is not founded on any pretended obligation, or antient convention; which muſt be null, as it cannot bind thoſe who did not exiſt at the time of its inſtitution; and unjuſt, as it would reduce men, in the ages following, to a herd of brutes, without any power of judging, or acting. The laws receive their force and authority from an oath of fidelity, either tacit, or expreſſed, which living ſubjects have ſworn to their ſovereign, in order to reſtrain the inteſtine fermentation of the private intereſts of individuals. From hence ſprings their true and natural authority. Who then is their lawful interpreter? The ſovereign, that is, the repreſentative of ſociety, and not the judge, whoſe office is only to examine, if a man have, or have not committed an action contrary to the laws.

In

In every criminal caufe the judge fhould reafon fyllogiftically. The *major* fhould be the general law; the *minor*, the conformity of the action, or its oppofition to the laws; the *conclufion*, liberty, or punifhment. If the judge be obliged by the imperfection of the laws, or chufes, to make any other, or more fyllogifms than this, it will be an introduction to uncertainty.

There is nothing more dangerous than the common axiom : *the fpirit of the laws is to be confidered*. To adopt it is to give way to the torrent of opinions. This may feem a paradox to vulgar minds, which are more ftrongly affected by the fmalleft diforder before their eyes, than by the moft pernicious, though remote, confequences produced by one falfe principle adopted by a nation.

Our knowledge is in proportion to the number of our ideas. The more complex thefe are, the greater is the variety of pofi-

tions

tions in which they may be confidered. Every man hath his own particular point of view, and at different times, fees the fame objects in very different lights. The fpirit of the laws will then be the refult of the good, or bad logic of the judge ; and this will depend on his good or bad digeftion ; on the violence of his paffions ; on the rank, and condition of the accufed, or on his connections with the judge ; and on all thofe little circumftances, which change the appearance of objects in the fluctuating mind of man. Hence we fee the fate of a delinquent changed many times in paf-fing through the different courts of judica-ture, and his life and liberty, victims to the falfe ideas, or ill humour of the judge ; who miftakes the vague refult of his own confufed reafoning, for the juft interpreta-tion of the laws. We fee the fame crimes punifhed in a different manner at different times in the fame tribunals ; the confe-quence of not having confulted the con-ftant, and invariable voice of the laws, but the erring inftability of arbitrary in-terpretation. 20

THE

THE diforders, that may arife from a rigorous obfervance of the letter of penal laws, are not to be compared with thofe produced by the interpretation of them. The firft are temporary inconveniences which will oblige the legiflator to correct the letter of the law, the want of precifenefs, and uncertainty of which has occafioned thefe diforders; and this will put a ftop to the fatal liberty of explaining; the fource of arbitrary and venal declamations. When the code of laws is once fixed, it fhould be obferved in the literal fenfe, and nothing more is left to the judge, than to determine, whether an action be, or be not conformable to the written law. When the rule of right which ought to direct the actions of the philofopher, as well as the ignorant, is a matter of controverfy, not of fact, the people are flaves to the magiftrates. The defpotifm of this multitude of tyrants, is more infupportable, the lefs the diftance is between the oppreffor and the oppreffed; more fatal than that of one, for the tyranny of many is not to be fhaken off, but by

having

having recourfe to that of one alone. It is more cruel, as it meets with more oppofition, and the cruelty of a tyrant is not in proportion to his ftrength, but to the obftacles that oppofe him.

THESE are the means, by which fecurity of perfon and property is beft obtained; which is juft, as it is the purpofe of uniting in fociety; and it is ufeful, as each perfon may calculate exactly the inconveniences attending every crime. By thefe means, fubjects will acquire a fpirit of independance and liberty; however it may appear to thofe, who dare to call the weaknefs of fubmitting blindly to their capricious and interefted opinions, by the facred name of virtue.

THESE principles will difpleafe thofe, who have made it a rule with themfelves, to tranfmit to their inferiors the tyranny they fuffer from their fuperiors. I fhould have every thing to fear, if tyrants were to read my book; but tyrants never read. 21

C   CHAP.

CHAP. V.

Of the Obscurity of Laws.

IF the power of interpreting laws be an
evil, obscurity in them must be another,
as the former is the consequence of the
latter. This evil will be still greater, if
the laws be written in a language unknown to the people; who, being ignorant
of the consequences of their own actions,
become necessarily dependant on a few,
who are interpreters of the laws, which,
instead of being public, and general, are
thus rendered private, and particular.
What must we think of mankind, when
we reflect, that such is the established
custom of the greatest part of our polished,
and enlightened Europe? Crimes will be
less frequent, in proportion as the code
of laws is more universally read, and understood; for there is no doubt, but that
the eloquence of the passions is greatly
assisted by the ignorance, and uncertainty
of punishments.

HENCE

HENCE it follows, that without written laws, no society will ever acquire a fixed form of government, in which the power is vested in the whole, and not in any part of the society; and in which, the laws are not to be altered, but by the will of the whole, nor corrupted by the force of private interest. Experience and reason shews us, that the probability of human traditions diminishes in proportion as they are distant from their sources. How then can laws resist the inevitable force of time, if there be not a lasting monument of the social compact?

HENCE, we see the use of printing, which alone makes the public, and not a few individuals, the guardians and defenders of the laws. It is this art, which, by diffusing literature, has gradually dissipated the gloomy spirit of cabal and intrigue. To this art it is owing, that the atrocious crimes of our ancestors, who were alternately slaves, and tyrants, are become less frequent. Those who are acquainted with the history of the two or

three

three laſt centuries, may obſerve, how, from the lap of luxury and effeminacy, have ſprung the moſt tender virtues, humanity, benevolence, and toleration of human errors. They may contemplate the effects of, what was ſo improperly called, ancient ſimplicity, and good faith ; humanity groaning under implacable ſuperſtition ; the avarice and ambition of a few, ſtaining, with human blood, the thrones and palaces of kings; ſecret treaſons, and public maſſacres; every noble a tyrant over the people; and the miniſters of the goſpel of Chriſt, bathing their hands in blood, in the name of the God of all mercy. We may talk as we pleaſe of the corruption and degeneracy of the preſent age, but happily we ſee no ſuch horrid examples of cruelty and oppreſſion.

CHAP.

CHAP. VI.

Of the Proportion between Crimes and Punishments.

IT is not only the common interest of mankind, that crimes should not be committed, but that crimes of every kind should be less frequent, in proportion to the evil they produce to society. Therefore, the means made use of by the legislature to prevent crimes, should be more powerful, in proportion as they are destructive of the public safety and happiness, and as the inducements to commit them are stronger. Therefore there ought to be a fixed proportion between crimes and punishments.

IT is impossible to prevent entirely all the disorders which the passions of mankind cause in society.[24] These disorders increase in proportion to the number of people, and the opposition of private interests. If we consult history, we shall find them

C 3   increasing,

increafing, in every ftate, with the extent
of dominion. In political arithmetic, it is
neceffary to fubftitute a calculation of pro-
babilities, to mathematical exactnefs. That
force, which continually impels us to our
own private intereft, like gravity, acts inceffantly, unlefs it meets with an obftacle
to oppofe it. The effects of this force are
the confufed feries of human actions. Punifhments, which I would call political
obftacles, prevent the fatal effects of private
intereft, without deftroying the impelling
caufe, which is that fenfibility infeparable
from man. The legiflator acts, in this cafe,
like a fkilful architect, who endeavours to
counteract the force of gravity, by combining the circumftances which may contribute to the ftrength of his edifice.

THE neceffity of uniting in fociety being granted, together with the conventions, which the oppofite interefts of individuals muft neceffarily require, a fcale of
crimes may be formed, of which the firft
degree fhould confift of thofe, which immediately tend to the diffolution of fociety,
and

and the last, of the smallest possible injustice done to a private member of that society. Between these extremes will be comprehended, all actions contrary to the public good, which are called criminal, and which descend by insensible degrees, decreasing from the highest to the lowest. If mathematical calculation could be applied to the obscure and infinite combinations of human actions, there might be a corresponding scale of punishments, descending from the greatest to the least; but it will be sufficient that the wise legislator mark the principal divisions, without disturbing the order, left to crimes of the *first* degree, be assigned punishments of the *last*. If there were an exact and universal scale of crimes and punishments, we should there have a common measure of the degree of liberty and slavery, humanity and cruelty of different nations.

Any action, which is not comprehended in the above-mentioned scale, will not be called a crime, or punished as such, except by those who have an interest in the deno-

mination.

mination. The uncertainty of the extreme points of this scale, hath produced a system of morality which contradicts the laws; a multitude of laws that contradict each other; and many, which expose the best men to the severest punishments, rendering the ideas of *vice* and *virtue* vague and fluctuating, and even their existence doubtful. Hence that fatal lethargy of political bodies, which terminates in their destruction.

WHOEVER reads, with a philosophic eye, the history of nations, and their laws, will generally find, that the ideas of virtue and vice, of a good or a bad citizen, change with the revolution of ages; not in proportion to the alteration of circumstances, and consequently conformable to the common good; but in proportion to the passions and errors by which the different law-givers were successively influenced. He will frequently observe, that the passions and vices of one age, are the foundation of the morality of the following; that violent passion, the offspring of fanaticism and enthusiasm, being weakened by time, which reduces all

the

the phenomena of the natural and moral world to an equality, become, by degrees, the prudence of the age, and an useful inftrument in the hands of the powerful, or artful politician.   Hence the uncertainty of our notions of honour and virtue; an uncertainty which will ever remain, becaufe they change with the revolutions of time, and names furvive the things they originally fignified; they change with the boundaries of ftates, which are often the fame both in phyfical and moral geography.

P L E A S U R E and pain are the only fprings of action in beings endowed with fenfibility.   Even amongft the motives which incite men to acts of religion, the invifible legiflator has ordained rewards and punifhments.   From a partial diftribution of thefe, will arife that contradiction, fo little obferved, becaufe fo common; I mean, that of punifhing by the laws, the crimes which the laws have occafioned. If an equal punifhment be ordained for two crimes that injure fociety in different de-

grees,

grees, there is nothing to deter men from committing the greater, as often as it is attended with greater advantage.

C H A P. VII.

Of estimating the Degree of Crimes.

THE foregoing reflections authorise me to assert, that crimes are only to be measured by the injury done to society.

THEY err, therefore, who imagine, that a crime is greater or less, according to the intention of the person by whom it is committed; for this will depend on the actual impression of objects on the senses, and on the previous disposition of the mind; both which will vary in different persons, and even in the same person at different times, according to the succession of ideas, passions, and circumstances. Upon that system, it would be necessary to form, not only a particular code for every individual, but a new penal law for every crime. Men, often with the best intention, do the greatest in-

jury

jury to fociety, and with the worft do it the moft effential fervices.

OTHERS have eftimated crimes rather by the dignity of the perfon offended, than by their confequences to fociety. If this were the true ftandard, the fmalleft irreverence to the divine Being ought to be punifhed with infinitely more feverity, than the affaffination of a monarch.

IN fhort, others have imagined, that the greatnefs of the fin fhould aggravate the crime. But the fallacy of this opinion will appear on the flighteft confideration of the relations between man and man, and between God and man. The relations between man and man are relations of equality. Neceffity alone hath produced, from the oppofition of private paffions and interefts, the idea of public utility, which is the foundation of human juftice. The other are relations of dependance, between an imperfect creature and his Creator, the moft perfect of beings, who has referved to himfelf the fole right of being both law-
giver,

giver, and judge; for he alone can, without
injuſtice, be, at the ſame time, both one
and the other.   If he hath decreed eternal
puniſhments for thoſe who diſobey his
will, ſhall an inſect dare to put himſelf in
the place of divine juſtice, or pretend to
puniſh for the Almighty, who is himſelf
all ſufficient; who cannot receive impreſſions of pleaſure, or pain, and who alone,
of all other beings, acts without being
acted upon ? The degree of ſin depends on
the malignity of the heart, which is impenetrable to finite beings.   How then can
the degree of ſin ſerve as a ſtandard to determine the degree of crimes ? If that
were admitted, men may puniſh when God
pardons, and pardon when God condemns;
and thus act in oppoſition to the ſupreme
Being.

CHAP.

C H A P.   VIII.

Of the Divifion of Crimes.

WE have proved, then, that crimes are to be eftimated by *the injury done to fociety*. This is one of thofe palpable truths, which, though evident to the meaneft capacity, yet, by a combination of circumftances, are only known to a few thinking men in every nation, and in every age. But opinions, worthy only of the defpotifm of Afia, and paffions, armed with power and authority, have, generally by infenfible, and fometimes by violent impreffions on the timid credulity of men, effaced thofe fimple ideas, which perhaps conftituted the firft philofophy of infant fociety. Happily the philofophy of the prefent enlightened age feems again to conduct us to the fame principles, and with that degree of certainty, which is obtained by a rational examination, and repeated experience

A SCRU-

A SCRUPULOUS adherence to order would require, that we fhould now examine and diftinguifh the different fpecies of crimes, and the modes of punifhment; but they are fo variable in their nature, from the different circumftances of ages, and countries, that the detail would be tirefome and endlefs. It will be fufficient for my purpofe to point out the moft general principles, and the moft common and dangerous errors, in order to undeceive, as well thofe who, from a miftaken zeal for liberty, would introduce anarchy and confufion, as thofe, who pretend to reduce fociety in general to the regularity of a convent.

SOME crimes are immediately deftructive of fociety, or its reprefentative; others attack the private fecurity of the life, property, or honour of individuals; and a third clafs confifts of fuch actions, as are contrary to the laws which relate to the general good of the community.

THE

THE firſt, which are of the higheſt degree, as they are moſt deſtructive to ſo-
ſociety, are called crimes of *Leze-majeſty.*
Tyranny, and ignorance, which have confounded the cleareſt terms and ideas, have
given this appellation to crimes of a different nature, and conſequently have eſtabliſhed the ſame puniſhment for each ; and
on this occaſion, as on a thouſand others,
men have been ſacrificed, victims to a
word. Every crime, even of the moſt private nature, injures ſociety; but every crime
does not threaten its immediate deſtruction.
Moral, as well as phyſical actions, have
their ſphere of activity differently circum-
ſcribed, like all the movements of nature,
by time and ſpace; it is therefore a ſophi-
ſtical interpretation, the common philoſophy of ſlaves, that would confound the
limits of things, eſtabliſhed by eternal
truth.

To theſe ſucceed crimes which are
deſtructive of the ſecurity of individuals.
This ſecurity being the principal end of
all

High-Treaſon.

all fociety, and to which every citizen
hath an undoubted right, it becomes in-
difpenfably neceffary, that to thefe crimes
the greateft of punifhments fhould be af-
figned.

THE opinion, that every member of
fociety has a right to do any thing, that is
not contrary to the laws, without fearing
any other inconveniences, than thofe which
are the natural confequences of the action
itfelf, is a political dogma, which fhould
be defended by the laws, inculcated by the
magiftrates, and believed by the people; a
facred dogma, without which there can be
no lawful fociety; a juft recompence for
our facrifice of that univerfal liberty of action, common to all fenfible beings, and
only limited by our natural powers. By
this principle our minds become free, active,
and vigorous; by this alone we are infpired
with that virtue which knows no fear, fo
different from that pliant prudence, worthy of thofe only who can bear a precarious exiftence.

AT-

ATTEMPTS, therefore, againſt the life, and liberty of a citizen, are crimes of the higheſt nature. Under this head we comprehend not only aſſaſſinations, and robberies, committed by the populace, but by grandees and magiſtrates; whoſe example acts with more force, and at a greater diſtance, deſtroying the ideas of juſtice and duty among the ſubjects, and ſubſtituting that of the right of the ſtrongeſt, equally dangerous to thoſe who exerciſe it, and to thoſe who ſuffer.

CHAP. IX.

Of Honour.

THERE is a remarkable difference between the civil laws, thoſe jealous guardians of life and property, and the laws of what is called *honour,* which particularly reſpects the opinion of others. Honour is a term, which has been the foundation of many long and brilliant reaſonings, without annexing to it any pre-

D   ciſe,

cife, or fixed idea. How miferable is the
condition of the human mind, to which
the moft diftant, and leaft effential matters, the revolutions of the heavenly bodies,
are more diftinctly known, than the moft
interefting truths of morality, which are
always confufed and fluctuating, as they
happen to be driven by the gales of paffion, or received and tranfmitted by ignorance! But this will ceafe to appear
ftrange, if it be confidered, that as objects, when too near the eye, appear confufed, fo the too great vicinity of the ideas
of morality, is the reafon why the fimple
ideas, of which they are compofed, are
eafily confounded; but which muft be
feparated, before we can inveftigate the
phenomena of human fenfibility; and the
intelligent obferver of human nature will
ceafe to be furprifed, that fo many ties,
and fuch an apparatus of morality, are
neceffary to the fecurity, and happinefs of
mankind.

Honour, then, is one of thofe complex ideas, which are an aggregate not
only

only of fimple ones, but of others fo complicated, that in their various modes of
affecting the human mind, they fometimes admit, and fometimes exclude part
of the elements of which they are compofed; retaining only fome few of the moft
common, as many algebraic quantities admit one common divifor. To find this
common divifor of the different ideas attached to the word honour, it will be neceffary to go back to the original formation
of fociety.

THE firft laws, and the firft magiftrates,
owed their exiftence to the neceffity of
preventing the diforders, which the natural defpotifm of individuals would una-
voidably produce. This was the object of
the eftablifhment of fociety, and was either
in reality, or in appearance, the principal defign of all codes of laws, even the
moft pernicious. But the more intimate
connections of men, and the progrefs of
their knowledge, gave rife to an infinite
number of neceffities, and mutual acts of
friendfhip, between the members of fociety.

D 2   Thefe

Thefe neceffities were not forefeen by the laws, and could not be fatisfied by the actual power of each individual. At this epocha began to be eftablifhed the defpotifm of opinion, as being the only means of obtaining thofe benefits, which the law could not procure, and of removing thofe evils, againft which the laws were no fecurity. It is opinion, that tormentor of the wife, and the ignorant, that has exalted the appearance of virtue above virtue itfelf. Hence the efteem of men becomes not only ufeful, but neceffary to every one, to prevent his finking below the common level. The ambitious man grafps at it, as being neceffary to his defigns ; the vain man fues for it, as a teftimony of his merit ; the honeft man demands it, as his due ; and moft men confider it as neceffary to their exiftence.

Honour, being produced after the formation of fociety, could not be a part of the common depofite, and therefore, whilft we act under its influence, we return, for that inftant, to a ftate of nature, and with-
draw

draw ourselves from the laws, which, in this case, are insufficient for our protection.

HENCE it follows, that in extreme political liberty, and in absolute despotism, all ideas of honour disappear, or are confounded with others. In the first case, reputation becomes useless from the despotism of the laws; and in the second, the despotism of one man, annulling all civil existence, reduces the rest to a precarious and temporary personality. Honour then is one of the fundamental principles of those monarchies, which are a limited despotism, and in these, like revolutions in despotic states, it is a momentary return to a state of nature, and original equality.

D 3   CHAP.

CHAP. X.

Of Duelling.

FROM the neceffity of the efteem of others, have arifen fingle combats, and they have been eftablifhed by the anarchy of the laws. They are thought to have been unknown to the ancients ; perhaps becaufe they did not affemble in their temples, in their theatres, or with their friends, fufpicioufly armed with fwords ; and, perhaps, becaufe fingle combats were a common fpectacle, exhibited to the people by gladiators, who were flaves, and whom freemen difdained to imitate.

In vain have the laws endeavoured to abolifh this cuftom, by punifhing the offenders with death. A man of honour, deprived of the efteem of others, forefees that he muft be reduced, either to a folitary exiftence, infupportable to a focial creature, or become the object of perpetual infult ;

fiderations fufficient to overcome the fear
of death.

WHAT is the reafon, that duels are
not fo frequent among the common people,
as amongft the great? Not only becaufe
they do not wear fwords, but becaufe, to
men of that clafs, reputation is of lefs
importance, than it is to thofe of a higher
rank, who commonly regard each other
with diftruft and jealoufy.

IT may not be without its ufe to repeat
here, what has been mentioned by other
writers; *viz.* that the beft method of preventing this crime is to punifh the aggref-
for, that is, the perfon who gave occafion
to the duel, and to acquit him, who, without any fault on his fide, is obliged to defend that, which is not fufficiently fecured
to him by the laws.

D 4   CHAP.

CHAP. XI.

Of Crimes, which disturb the public Tranquillity.

ANOTHER class of crimes are those which disturb the public tranquillity and the quiet of the citizens; such as tumults and riots in the public streets, which are intended for commerce and the passage of the inhabitants; the discourses of fanatics, which rouse the passions of the curious multitude, and gain strength from the number of their hearers, who, though deaf to calm and solid reasoning, are always affected by obscure and mysterious enthusiasm.

THE illumination of the streets, during the night, at the public expence; guards stationed in different quarters of the city; the plain and moral discourses of religion, reserved for the silence and tranquillity of churches, and protected by authority; and

harangues

harangues in support of the interest of the public, delivered only at the general meetings of the nation, in parliament, or where the sovereign resides; are all means to prevent the dangerous effects of the misguided passions of the people. These should be the principal objects of the vigilance of a magistrate, and which the French call *Police*; but if this magistrate should act in an arbitrary manner, and not in conformity to the code of laws, which ought to be in the hands of every member of the community, he opens a door to tyranny, which always surrounds the confines of political liberty.

I do not know of any exception to this general axiom, that *Every member of society should know when he is criminal, and when innocent.*[27] If censors, and, in general, arbitrary magistrates, be necessary in any government, it proceeds from some fault in the constitution. The uncertainty of crimes hath sacrificed more victims to secret tyranny, than have ever suffered by public and solemn cruelty.

WHAT

WHAT are, in general, the proper punishments for crimes? Is the punishment of death really *useful*, or necessary for the safety or good order of society? Are tortures and torments consistent with *justice*, or do they answer the *end* proposed by the laws? Which is the best method of preventing crimes? Are the same punishments equally useful at all times? What influence have they on manners? These problems should be solved with that geometrical precision, which the mist of sophistry, the seduction of eloquence, and the timidity of doubt, are unable to resist.

IF I have no other merit than that of having first presented to my country, with a greater degree of evidence, what other nations have written, and are beginning to practise, I shall account myself fortunate; but if, by supporting the rights of mankind and of invincible truth, I shall contribute to save from the agonies of death one unfortunate victim of tyranny, or of ignorance, equally fatal; his blessing and tears of transport, will be a sufficient con-

confolation to me for the contempt of all mankind.

C H A P.   XII.

Of the Intent of Punifhments.

FROM the foregoing confiderations it is evident, that the intent of punifhments, is not to torment a fenfible being, nor to undo a crime already committed. Is it poffible that torments and ufelefs cruelty, the inftrument of furious fanaticifm, or the impotency of tyrants, can be authorifed by a political body ? which, fo far from being influenced by paffion, fhould be the cool moderator of the paffions of individuals. Can the groans of a tortured wretch recall the time paft, or reverfe the crime he has committed ?

THE end of punifhment, therefore, is no other, than to prevent the criminal from doing further injury to fociety, and to prevent others from committing the like offence.

offence. Such punifhments, therefore, and
fuch a mode of inflicting them, ought to
be chofen, as will make the ftrongeft and
moft lafting impreffions on the minds of
others, with the leaft torment to the body
of the criminal.

CHAP. XIII.

Of the Credibility of Witneſſes.

TO determine exactly the credibility of
a witnefs, and the force of evidence,
is an important point in every good legiflation. Every man of common fenfe, that
is, every one whofe ideas have fome connexion with each other, and whofe fenfa-
tions are conformable to thofe of other
men, may be a witnefs; but the credibility of his evidence will be in proportion
as he is interefted in declaring or concealing the truth. Hence it appears, how
frivolous is the reafoning of thofe, who
reject the teftimony of women on account
of their weaknefs; how puerile it is, not

to

to admit the evidence of those who are under sentence of death, because they are dead in law; and how irrational to exclude persons branded with infamy: for in all these cases they ought to be credited, when they have no interest in giving false testimony.

THE credibility of a witness, then, should only diminish in proportion to the hatred, friendship, or connexions, subsisting between him and the delinquent.   One witness is not sufficient; for whilst the accused denies what the other affirms, truth remains suspended, and the right that every one has to be believed innocent, turns the balance in his favour.

THE credibility of a witness is the less, as the atrociousness of the crime is greater, from the improbability of its having been committed; as in cases of witchcraft, and acts of wanton cruelty. ᵞ The writers on penal laws have adopted a contrary principle, viz. that the credibility of a witness is greater, as the crime is more atrocious.
                                                    Behold

Behold their inhuman maxim, dictated by the moft cruel imbecility. *In atrociffimis, leviores conjecturæ fufficiunt & licet judici jura tranfgredi.* Let us tranflate this fentence, that mankind may fee one of the many unreafonable principles to which they are ignorantly fubject. *In the moft atrocious crimes the flighteft conjectures are fufficient, and the judge is allowed to exceed the limits of the law.* The abfurd practices of legiflators, are often the effect of timidity, which is a principal fource of the contradictions of mankind. The legiflators, (or rather lawyers, whofe opinions, when alive, were interefted and venal, but which after their death become of decifive authority, and are the fovereign arbiters of the lives and fortunes of men) terrified by the condemnation of fome innocent perfon, have burthened the law with pompous and ufelefs formalities, the fcrupulous obfervance of which will place annarchical impunity on the throne of juftice; at other times, perplexed by atrocious crimes of difficult proof, they imagined themfelves under a neceffity of fuperceding the very formalities eftablifhed

blifhed by themfelves; and thus, at one
time, with defpotic impatience, and at another with feminine timidity, they transform their folemn judgments into a game
of hazard.

But to return.   In the cafe of witchcraft, it is much more probable, that a number of men fhould be deceived, than that
any perfon fhould exercife a power which
God hath refufed to every created being.
In like manner, in cafes of wanton cruelty,
the prefumption is always againft the ac-
cufer, for no man is cruel without fome intereft, without fome motive of fear or hate.
There are no fpontaneous or fuperfluous
fentiments in the heart of man; they are
all the refult of impreffions on the fenfes.

The credibility of a witnefs may alfo
be diminifhed, by his being a member of a
private fociety, whofe cuftoms and principles of conduct are either not known, or
are different from thofe of the public.
Such a man has not only his own paffions,
but

but thofe of the fociety of which he is a member. [29]

FINALLY, the credibility of a witnefs is null, when the queftion relates to the words of a criminal ; for the tone of voice, the gefture, all that precedes, accompanies and follows, the different ideas which men annex to the fame words, may fo alter and modify a man's difcourfe, that it is almoft impoffible to repeat them precifely in the manner in which they were fpoken. Befides, violent and uncommon actions, fuch as real crimes, leave a trace in the multitude of circumftances that attend them, and in their effects ; but words remain only in the memory of the hearers, who are commonly negligent or prejudiced. It is infinitely eafier then to found an accufation on the words, than on the actions of a man ; for in thefe, the number of circumftances, urged againft the accufed, afford him variety of means of juftification.

CHAP,

CHAP. XIV

Of Evidence and the Proofs of a Crime, and of the Form of Judgment.

THE following general theorem is of great use in determining the certainty of a fact. When the proofs of a crime are dependant on each other, that is, when the evidence of each witness, taken separately, proves nothing; or when all the proofs are dependant upon one, the number of proofs neither increase nor diminish the probability of the fact; for the force of the whole is no greater than the force of that on which they depend; and if this fails, they all fall to the ground. When the proofs are independant on each other, the probability of the fact increases in proportion to the number of proofs; for the falshood of one does not diminish the veracity of another.

It may seem extraordinary, that I speak of probability with regard to crimes, which, to deserve a punishment, must be certain.

E   But

But this paradox will vanish, when it is considered, that, strictly speaking, moral certainty is only probability; but which is called a certainty, because every man in his senses assents to it from an habit produced by the necessity of acting, and which is anterior to all speculation. That certainty which is necessary to decide, that the accused is guilty, is the very same which determines every man in the most important transactions of his life.

The proofs of a crime may be divided into two classes, perfect and imperfect. I call those perfect which exclude the possibility of innocence; imperfect, those which do not exclude this possibility. Of the first, one only is sufficient for condemnation; of the second, as many are required as form a perfect proof; that is to say, that though each of these, separately taken, does not exclude the possibility of innocence, it is nevertheless excluded by their union. It should be also observed, that the imperfect proofs, of which the accused, if innocent,
cent,

cent, might clear himfelf, and does not, become perfect.

BUT it is much eafier to feel this moral certainty of proofs, than to define it exactly. For this reafon, I think it an excellent law which eftablifhes affiftants to the principal judge, and thofe chofen by lot; for that ignorance, which judges by its feelings, is lefs fubject to error, than the knowledge of the laws, which judges by opinion. Where the laws are clear and precife, the office of the judge is merely to afcertain the fact. If, in examining the proofs of a crime, acutenefs and dexterity be required; if clearnefs and precifion be neceffary in fumming up the refult; to judge of the refult itfelf, nothing is wanting but plain and ordinary good fenfe; a lefs fallacious guide than the knowledge of a judge, accuftomed to find guilty, and to reduce all things to an artificial fyftem, borrowed from his ftudies. Happy the nation, where the knowledge of the law is not a fcience!

E 2   IT

IT is an admirable law which ordains, that every man fhall be tried by his peers ; for when life, liberty and fortune are in queftion, the fentiments, which a difference of rank and fortune infpire, fhould be filent ; that fuperiority with which the fortunate look upon the unfortunate, and that envy with which the inferior regard their fuperiors, fhould have no influence. But when the crime is an offence againft a fellow fubject, one half of the judges fhould be peers to the accufed, and the other, peers to the perfon offended. So that all private intereft, which, in fpite of ourfelves, modifies the appearance of objects, even in the eyes of the moft equitable, is counteracted, and nothing remains to turn afide the direction of truth and the laws. It is alfo juft, that the accufed fhould have the liberty of excluding a certain number of his judges. Where this liberty is enjoyed for a long time, without any inftance to the contrary, the criminal feems to condemn himfelf.

ALL

ALL trials fhould be public, that opinion, which is the beft, or perhaps, the
only cement of fociety, may curb the authority of the powerful, and the paffions
of the judge; and that the people may
fay, "We are protected by the laws; we
"are not flaves:" a fentiment which infpires courage, and which is the beft tribute to a fovereign, who knows his real
intereft. I fhall not enter into particulars. There may be fome perfons who
expect that I fhould fay all that can be
faid upon this fubject; to fuch, what I
have already written muft be unintel-
ligible.

CHAP. XV.

Of fecret Accufations.

SECRET accufations are a manifeft
abufe, but confecrated by cuftom in
many nations, where, from the weaknefs
of the government, they are neceffary.
This cuftom makes men falfe and treacherous. Whoever fufpects another to be an

E 3   in-

informer, beholds in him an enemy ; and
from thence, mankind are accuftomed to
difguife their real fentiments ; and from
the habit of concealing them from others,
they at laft even hide them from themfelves. Unhappy are thofe, who have arrived at this point! Without any certain
and fixed principles to guide them, they
fluctuate in the vaft fea of opinion, and are
bufied only in efcaping the monfters which
furround them; to thofe, the prefent is
always embittered by the uncertainty of
the future ; deprived of the pleafures of
tranquillity and fecurity, fome fleeting moments of happinefs, fcattered thinly through
their wretched lives, confole them for the
mifery of exifting. Shall we, amongft fuch
men, find intrepid foldiers, to defend their
king and country? Amongft fuch men,
fhall we find incorruptible magiftrates, who,
with the fpirit of freedom and patriotic
eloquence, will fupport and explain the
true intereft of their fovereign ; who, with
the tributes, offer up at the throne the love
and blefling of the people, and thus beftow
on the palaces of the great and the humble
                                    cottage,

cottage, peace and security; and to the in-
dustrious a prospect of bettering their lot,
that useful ferment and vital principle of
states ?

WHO can defend himself from calumny,
armed with that impenetrable shield of
tyranny, secrecy ? What a miserable government must that be, where the sovereign
suspects an enemy in every subject; and
to secure the tranquillity of the public, is
obliged to sacrifice the repose of every individual ?

BY what arguments is it pretended, that
secret accusations may be justified ! The
public safety, say they, and the security
and maintenance of the established form of
government.   But what a strange constitution is that, where the government, which
hath in its favour not only power, but opinion, still more efficacious, yet fears its
own subjects ? *The indemnity of the informer.*   Do not the laws defend him sufficiently ; and are there subjects more powerful than the laws? *The necessity of protecting*

the informer from infamy. Then fecret calumny is authorifed, and punifhed only
when public. *The nature of the crime.* If
actions, indifferent in themfelves, or even
ufeful to the public, were called crimes,
both the accufation and the trial could
never be too fecret. But can there be any
crime, committed againft the public, which
ought not to be publicly punifhed? I refpect all governments; and I fpeak not of
any one in particular. Such may fometimes be the nature of circumftances, that
when abufes are inherent in the conftitution, it may be imagined, that to rectify
them would be to deftroy the conftitution
itfelf. But were I to dictate new laws in
a remote corner of the univerfe, the good
of pofterity, ever prefent to my mind,
would hold back my trembling hand, and
prevent me from authorizing *fecret accufations.*

PUBLIC accufations, fays *Montefquieu,*
are more conformable to the nature of a
republic, where zeal for the public good is
the principal paffion of a citizen, than of a
monarchy,

monarchy, in which, as this fentiment is very feeble, from the nature of the government, the beft eftablifhment is that of *commiffioners*, who, in the name of the public, accufe the infractors of the laws. But in all governments, as well in a republic as in a monarchy, the punifhment, due to the crime of which one accufes another, ought to be inflicted on the informer.

C H A P. XVI.

Of Torture.

THE torture of a criminal, during the courfe of his trial, is a cruelty confecrated by cuftom in moft nations. It is ufed with an intent either to make him confefs his crime, or explain fome contradictions, into which he had been led during his examination; or difcover his accomplices; or for fome kind of metaphyfical and incomprehenfible purgation of infamy; or, finally, in order to difcover other crimes, of which he is not accufed, but of which he may be guilty.

No

No man can be judged a criminal until he be found guilty; nor can society take from him the public protection, until it have been proved that he has violated the conditions on which it was granted. What right then, but that of power, can authorize the punishment of a citizen, so long as there remains any doubt of his guilt? This dilemma is frequent. Either he is guilty, or not guilty. If guilty, he should only suffer the punishment ordained by the laws, and torture becomes useless, as his confession is unnecessary. If he be not guilty, you torture the innocent; for in the eye of the law, every man is innocent, whose crime has not been proved. Besides, it is confounding all relations, to expect that a man should be both the accuser and accused; and that pain should be the test of truth, as if truth resided in the muscles and fibres of a wretch in torture. By this method, the robust will escape, and the feeble be condemned. These are the inconveniences of this pretended test of truth, worthy only of a cannibal; and which the Romans, in many respects, barbarous, and whose savage virtue

virtue has been too much admired, referved for the flaves alone.

WHAT is the political intention of punifhments? To terrify, and be an example to others. Is this intention anfwered, by thus privately torturing the guilty and the innocent? It is doubtlefs of importance, that no crime fhould remain unpunifhed; but it is ufelefs to make a public example of the author of a crime hid in darknefs. A crime already committed, and for which there can be no remedy, can only be punifhed by a political fociety, with an intention, that no hopes of impunity fhould induce others to commit the fame. If it be true, that the number of thofe, who from fear or virtue refpect the laws, is greater than of thofe by whom they are violated, the rifk of torturing an innocent perfon is greater, as there is a greater probability, that, *cæteris paribus*, an individual hath obferved, than that he hath infringed the laws.

THERE

THERE is another ridiculous motive for torture, namely, *to purge a man from infamy.* Ought such an abuse to be tolerated in the eighteenth century ? Can pain, which is a sensation, have any connexion with a moral sentiment, a matter of opinion ? Perhaps the rack may be considered as the refiner's furnace.

IT is not difficult to trace this senseless law to its origin ; for an absurdity, adopted by a whole nation, must have some affinity with other ideas, established and respected by the same nation. This custom seems to be the offspring of religion, by which mankind, in all nations, and in all ages, are so generally influenced. We are taught by our infallible church, that those stains of sin, contracted through human frailty, and which have not deserved the eternal anger of the Almighty, are to be purged away, in another life, by an incomprehensible fire. Now infamy is a stain, and if the punishments and fire of purgatory can take away all spiritual stains, why should not the pain of torture take

away

away thofe of a civil nature ? I imagine,
that the confeffion of a criminal, which in
fome tribunals is required, as being effential to his condemnation, has a fimilar
origin, and has been taken from the myfterious tribunal of penitence, where the
confeffion of fins is a neceffary part of the
facrament. Thus have men abufed the un-
erring light of revelation ; and in the times
of tractable ignorance, having no other,
they naturally had recourfe to it on every
occafion, making the moft remote and abfurd applications. Moreover, infamy is a
fentiment regulated neither by the laws nor
by reafon, but entirely by opinion. But
torture renders the victim infamous, and
therefore cannot take infamy away.

ANOTHER intention of torture is, to
oblige the fuppofed criminal to reconcile
the contradictions into which he may have
fallen, during his examination ; as if the
dread of punifhment, the uncertainty of his
fate, the folemnity of the court, the ma-
jefty of the judge, and the ignorance of the
accufed, were not abundantly fufficient to
account

account for contradictions, which are fo
common to men, even in a ftate of tranquillity; and which muft neceffarily be multiplied by the perturbation of the mind of
a man, entirely engaged in the thoughts of
faving himfelf from imminent danger.

THIS infamous teft of truth is a remaining monument of that ancient and favage
legiflation, in which trials by fire, by boiling water, or the uncertainty of combats,
were called *Judgments of God*; as if the
links of that eternal chain, whofe beginning is in the breaft of the firft caufe of all
things, could ever be difunited by the inftitutions of men. The only difference between torture, and trials by fire and boiling
water is, that the event of the firft depends
on the will of the accufed; and of the
fecond, on a faft entirely phyfical and external: but this difference is apparent only,
not real. A man on the rack, in the con-
vulfions of torture, has it as little in his
power to declare the truth, as in former
times, to prevent without fraud the effects
of fire or boiling water.

EVERY

EVERY act of the will is invariably in proportion to the force of the impreffion on our fenfes. The impreffion of pain, then, may increafe to fuch a degree, that occupying the mind entirely, it will compel the fufferer to ufe the fhorteft method of freeing himfelf from torment. His anfwer, therefore, will be in effect, as neceffary as that of fire or boiling water; and he will accufe himfelf of crimes of which he is innocent. So that the very means employed to diftinguifh the innocent from the guilty, will moft effectually deftroy all difference between them.

IT would be fuperfluous to confirm thefe reflections by examples of innocent perfons, who, from the agony of torture, have confeffed themfelves guilty: innumerable inftances may be found in all nations, and in every age. How amazing that mankind have always neglected to draw the natural conclufion! Lives there a man, who, if he have carried his thoughts ever fo little beyond the neceffities of life, when he reflects on fuch cruelty, is not tempted to fly from
fociety,

society, and return to his natural state of independance?

THE result of torture, then, is a matter of calculation, and depends on the constition, which differs in every individual, and is in proportion to his strength and sensibility; so that to discover truth by this method is a problem, which may be better solved by a mathematician than a judge, and may be thus stated. *The force of the muscles, and the sensibility of the nerves of an innocent person being given, it is required to find the degree of pain necessary to make him confess himself guilty of a given crime.*

THE examination of the accused is intended to find out the truth; but if this be discovered, with so much difficulty, in the air, gesture, and countenance of a man at ease, how can it appear in a countenance distorted by the convulsions of torture. Every violent action destroys those small alterations in the features, which sometimes disclose the sentiments of the heart.

THESE

These truths were known to the Roman legiſlators, amongſt whom, as I have already obſerved, ſlaves only, who were not conſidered as citizens, were tortured. They are known to the Engliſh, a nation in which the progreſs of ſcience, ſupeſiority in commerce, riches and power, its natural conſequences, together with the numerous examples of virtue and courage, leave no doubt of the excellence of its laws.[32] They have been acknowledged in Sweden, where torture has been aboliſhed. They are known to one of the wiſeſt monarchs in Europe,[33] who, having ſeated philoſophy on the throne, by his beneficent legiſlation, has made his ſubjects free, though dependant on the laws; the only freedom that reaſonable men can deſire in the preſent ſtate of things. In ſhort, torture has not been thought neceſſary in the laws of armies, compoſed chiefly of the dregs of mankind, where its uſe ſhould ſeem moſt neceſſary. Strange phenomenon! that a ſet of men, hardened by ſlaughter, and familiar with blood, ſhould teach humanity to the ſons of peace.

F

It appears also, that these truths were known, though imperfectly, even to those by whom torture has been most frequently practised; for a confession made during torture is null, if it be not afterwards confirmed by an oath; which if the criminal refuses, he is tortured again. Some civilians, and some nations, permit this infamous *petitio principii* to be only three times repeated, and others leave it to the discretion of the judge; therefore of two men equally innocent, or equally guilty, the most robust and resolute will be acquitted, and the weakest and most pusillanimous will be condemned, in consequence of the following excellent method of reasoning. *I, the judge, must find some one guilty. Thou, who art a strong fellow, hast been able to resist the force of torment; therefore I acquit thee. Thou, being weaker, hast yielded to it; I therefore condemn thee. I am sensible that the confession, which was extorted from thee, has no weight; but if thou dost not confirm by oath what thou hast already confessed, I will have thee tormented again.*

A VERY

A VERY ſtrange, but neceſſary, conſequence of the uſe of torture, is, that the
caſe of the innocent is worſe than that of
the guilty. With regard to the firſt, either
he confeſſes the crime, which he has not
committed, and is condemned; or he is
acquitted, and has ſuffered a puniſhment
he did not deſerve. On the contrary, the
perſon, who is really guilty, has the moſt
favourable ſide of the queſtion; for if he
ſupports the torture with firmneſs and re-
ſolution, he is acquitted, and has gained,
having exchanged a greater puniſhment
for a leſs.

THE law, by which torture is authorized, ſays, *Men, be inſenſible to pain. Na-*
ture has indeed given you an irreſiſtible ſelf-
love, and an unalienable right of ſelf-preſerva-
tion; but I create in you a contrary ſentiment,
an heroical hatred of yourſelves. I command
you to accuſe yourſelves, and to declare the
truth, midſt the tearing of your fleſh, and the
diſlocation of your bones.

F 2   TOR-

TORTURE is ufed to difcover, whether the criminal be guilty of other crimes befides thofe of which he is accufed; which is equivalent to the following reafoning. *Thou art guilty of one crime, therefore it is poffible that thou mayft have committed a thoufand others; but the affair being doubtful, I muft try it by my criterion of truth. The laws order thee to be tormented, becaufe thou art guilty, becaufe thou mayft be guilty, and becaufe I chufe thou fhouldft be guilty.*

TORTURE is ufed to make the criminal difcover his accomplices; but if it has been demonftrated that it is not a proper means of difcovering truth, how can it ferve to difcover the accomplices, which is one of the truths required. Will not the man who accufes himfelf, yet more readily accufe others? Befides, is it juft to torment one man for the crime of another? May not the accomplices be found out by the examination of the witneffes, or of the criminal; from the evidence, or from the nature of the crime itfelf; in fhort, by all the means that have been ufed to prove

the

the guilt of the prifoner? The accomplices commonly fly, when their comrade
is taken. The uncertainty of their fate
condemns them to perpetual exile, and
frees fociety from the danger of further
injury; whilft the punifhment of the criminal, by deterring others, anfwers the
purpofe for which it was ordained,

C H A P. XVII.

Of pecuniary Punifhments.

THERE was a time when all punifhments were pecuniary. The crimes
of the fubjects were the inheritance of the
prince. An injury done to fociety was a
favour to the crown; and the fovereign
and magiftrates, thofe guardians of the
public fecurity, were interefted in the violation of the laws. Crimes were tried at
that time, in a court of exchequer, and
the caufe became a civil fuit between the
perfon accufed and the crown. The magiftrate then had other powers than were

necefſary

neceſſary for the public welfare, and the
criminal ſuffered other puniſhments than
the neceſſity of example required. The
judge was rather a collector for the crown,
an agent for the treaſury, than a protector
and miniſter of the laws. But, according
to this ſyſtem, for a man to confeſs himſelf guilty, was to acknowledge himſelf a
debtor to the crown; which was, and is
at preſent (the effects continuing after the
cauſes have ceaſed) the intent of all criminal cauſes. Thus, the criminal who
refuſes to confeſs his crime, though convicted by the moſt undoubted proofs, will
ſuffer a leſs puniſhment than if he had confeſſed; and he will not be put to the
torture to oblige him to confeſs other crimes
which he might have committed, as he
has not confeſſed the principal. But the
confeſſion being once obtained, the judge
becomes maſter of his body, and torments
him with a ſtudied formality, in order to
ſqueeze out of him all the profit poſſible.
Confeſſion then is allowed to be a con-
vincing proof, eſpecially when obtained by
the force of torture; at the ſame time that
an

an extrajudicial confeffion, when a man is at eafe and under no apprehenfion, is not fufficient for his condemnation.

ALL enquiries, which may ferve to clear up the fact, but which may weaken the pretenfions of the crown, are excluded. It was not from compaffion to the criminal, or from confiderations of humanity, that torments were fometimes fpared, but out of fear of lofing thofe rights, which at prefent appear chimerical and inconceivable. The judge becomes an enemy to the accufed, to a wretch; a prey to the horrors of a dungeon, to torture, to death; and an uncertain futurity, more terrible than all; he inquires not into the truth of the fact, but the nature of the crime; he lays fnares to make him convict himfelf; he fears, left he fhould not fucceed in finding him guilty, and left that infallability, which every man arrogates to himfelf, fhould be called in queftion. It is in the power of the magiftrate to determine, what evidence is fufficient to fend a man to prifon; that he may be proved innocent, he muft firft

F 4   be

be fuppofed guilty. This is what is called an *offenfive* profecution; and fuch are all criminal proceedings, in the eighteenth century, in all parts of our polifhed Europe. The true profecution, *for information*; that is, an impartial inquiry into the fact, that which reafon prefcribes, which military laws adopt, and which Afiatic defpotifm allow in fuits of one fubject againft another, is very little practifed in any courts of juftice. What a labyrinth of abfurdities! Abfurdities, which will appear incredible to happier pofterity. The philofopher only will be able to read, in the nature of man, the poffibility of there ever having been fuch a fyftem.

CHAP. XVIII.

Of Oaths.

THERE is a palpable contradiction between the laws and the natural fentiments of mankind, in the cafe of *oaths*, which are adminiftred to a criminal to make him fpeak the truth, when the contrary is

his

his greateft intereft.   As if a man could think himfelf obliged to contribute to his own deftruction; and as if, when intereft fpeaks, religion was not generally filent; religion, which in all ages hath, of all other things, been moft commonly abufed; and indeed, upon what motive fhould it be refpected by the wicked, when it has been thus violated by thofe who were efteemed the wifeft of men? The motives which religion oppofes to the fear of impending evil; and the love of life, are too weak, as they are too diftant, to make any impref-fion on the fenfes.   The affairs of the other world are regulated by laws intirely diffe-rent from thofe by which human affairs are directed; why then fhould you endeavour to compromife matters between them? Why fhould a man be reduced to the ter-rible alternative, either of offending God, or of contributing to his own immediate deftruction? The laws which require an oath in fuch a cafe, leave him only the choice of becoming a bad chriftian, or a martyr. For this reafon, oaths become, by degrees, a mere formality, and all fenti-
                                ments

ments of religion, perhaps the only motive of honefty in the greateft part of mankind, are deftroyed. Experience proves their inutility; I appeal to every judge, whether he has ever known that an oath alone has brought truth from the lips of a criminal; and reafon tells us it muft be fo; for all laws are ufelefs, and in confequence, deftructive, which contradict the natural feelings of mankind. Such laws are like a dike oppofed directly to the courfe of a torrent; it is either immediately overwhelmed, or, by a whirlpool formed by itfelf, it is gradually undermined and deftroyed.[36]

C H A P. XIX.

Of the Advantage of immediate Punifhment.

THE more immediately after the commiffion of a crime, a punifhment is inflicted, the more juft and ufeful it will be. It will be more juft, becaufe it fpares the criminal the cruel and fuperfluous torment of uncertainty, which increafes in
proportion

proportion to the strength of his imagination and the sense of his weakness; and because the privation of liberty, being a punishment, ought to be inflicted before condemnation, but for as short a time as possible. Imprisonment, I say, being only the means of securing the person of the accused, until he be tried, condemned, or acquitted, ought not only to be of as short duration, but attended with as little severity as possible. The time should be determined by the necessary preparation for the trial, and the right of priority in the oldest prisoners. The confinement ought not to be closer than is requisite to prevent his flight, or his concealing the proofs of the crime; and the trial should be conducted with all possible expedition. Can there be a more cruel contrast than that between the indolence of a judge, and the painful anxiety of the accused; the comforts and pleasures of an insensible magistrate, and the filth and misery of the prisoner? In general, as I have before observed, *The degree of the punishment, and the consequences of a crime, ought to be so contrived, as to*

have

have the greatest possible effect on others, with the least possible pain to the delinquent. If there be any society in which this is not a fundamental principle, it is an unlawful society; for mankind, by their union, originally intended to subject themselves to the least evils possible.

An immediate punishment is more useful; because the smaller the interval of time between the punishment and the crime, the stronger and more lasting will be the association of the two ideas of *Crime* and *Punishment*; so that they may be considered, one as the cause, and the other as the unavoidable and necessary effect. It is demonstrated, that the association of ideas is the cement which unites the fabric of the human intellect; without which, pleasure and pain would be simple and ineffectual sensations. The vulgar, that is, all men, who have no general ideas, or universal principles, act in consequence of the most immediate and familiar associations; but the more remote and complex only present themselves to the minds of those who are

passionately

paffionately attached to a fingle object; or
to thofe of greater underftanding, who
have acquired an habit of rapidly comparing together a number of objects, and
of forming a conclufion; and the refult,
that is, the action in confequence, by
thefe means, becomes lefs dangerous and
uncertain.

IT is, then, of the greateft importance,
that the punifhment fhould fucceed the
crime as immediately as poffible, if we
intend, that in the rude minds of the multitude, the feducing picture of the advantage arifing from the crime, fhould inftantly
awake the attendant idea of punifhment.
Delaying the punifhment ferves only to
feparate thefe two ideas; and thus affects
the minds of the fpectators rather as being
a terrible fight, than the neceffary confequence of a crime; the horror of which
fhould contribute to heighten the idea of
the punifhment.

THERE is another excellent method of
ftrengthening this important connexion
between

between the ideas of crime and punifhment; that is, to make the punifhment
as analogous as poffible to the nature of
the crime; in order that the punifhment
may lead the mind to confider the crime
in a different point of view, from that, in
which it was placed by the flattering idea
of promifed advantages.

CRIMES of lefs importance are commonly punifhed, either in the obfcurity
of a prifon, or the criminal is *tranfported*,
to give, by his flavery, an example to focieties which he never offended; an example abfolutely ufelefs, becaufe diftant from
the place where the crime was committed.
Men do not, in general, commit great
crimes deliberately, but rather in a fudden
guft of paffion; and they commonly look
on the punifhment due to a great crime as
remote and improbable. The public punifhment, therefore, of fmall crimes, will
make a greater impreffion, and, by deter-
ing men from the fmaller, will effectually
prevent the greater.

CHAP.

CHAP. XX.

Of Acts of Violence.

SOME crimes relate to *perfon*, others to *property*. The firft ought to be punifhed corporally.   The great and rich fhould by no means have it in their power to fet a price on the fecurity of the weak and indigent; for then, riches, which under the protection of the laws, are the reward of induftry, would become the aliment of tyranny. Liberty is at an end, whenever the laws permit, that, in certain cafes, a man may ceafe to be *a perfon*, and become *a thing*. Then will the powerful employ their addrefs, to felect from the various combinations of civil fociety, all that is in their own favour. This is that magic art which transforms fubjects into beafts of burthen, and which, in the hands of the ftrong, is the chain that binds the weak and incautious. Thus it is, that in fome governments, where there is all the appearance of liberty, tyranny lies concealed, and infinuates itfelf into fome
neglected

neglected corner of the conftitution, where it gathers ftrength infenfibly. Mankind generally oppofe, with refolution, the af- faults of barefaced and open tyranny; but difregard the little infect that gnaws through the dike, and opens a fure, though fecret paffage to inundation.

CHAP. XXI.

Of the Punifhment of the Nobles.

WHAT punifhments fhall be ordained for the nobles, whofe privileges make fo great a part of the laws of nations? I do not mean to enquire whether the hereditary diftinction between nobles and commoners be ufeful in any government, or neceffary in a monarchy; or whether it be true, that they form an intermediate power, of ufe in moderating the exceffes of both extremes; or whether they be not rather flaves to their own body, and to others, confining within a very fmall circle the natural effects and hopes of induftry, like thofe little fruitful fpots, fcattered here and

and there in the fandy defarts of Arabia;
or whether it be true, that a fubordination
of rank and condition is inevitable, or ufeful in fociety; and if fo, whether this
fubordination fhould not rather fubfift between individuals, than particular bodies;
whether it fhould not rather circulate
through the whole body politic, than be
confined to one part; and rather than be
perpetual, fhould it not be inceffantly produced and deftroyed. Be thefe as they may,
I affert that the punifhment of a nobleman
fhould in no wife differ from that of the
loweft member of fociety.

Every lawful diftinction, either in honours or riches, fuppofes previous equality,
founded on the laws, on which all the
members of fociety are confidered as being
equally dependant. We fhould fuppofe
that men, in renouncing their natural defpotifm, faid, *the wifeft and moft induftrious
among us fhould obtain the greateft honours,
and his dignity fhall defcend to his pofterity.
The fortunate and happy, may hope for
greater honours, but let him not therefore be*
G   *lefs*

less afraid, than others, of violating those conditions on which he is exalted. It is true indeed that no such decrees were ever made in a general diet of mankind, but they exist in the invariable relations of things; nor do they destroy the advantages, which are supposed to be produced by the class of nobles, but prevent the inconveniences; and they make the laws respectable by destroying all hopes of impunity.

It may be objected, that the same punishment inflicted on a nobleman and a plebeian, becomes really different from the difference of their education, and from the infamy it reflects on an illustrious family; but I answer, that punishments are to be estimated, not by the sensibility of the criminal, but by the injury done to society; which injury is augmented by the high rank of the offender.[37] The precise equality of a punishment can never be more than external, as it is in proportion to the degree of sensibility, which differs in every individual. The infamy of an innocent family may be easily obliterated

by

by some public demonstration of favour from the sovereign; and forms have always more influence than reason on the gazing multitude.

CHAP. XXII.

Of Robbery.

THE punishment of robbery, not accompanied with violence, should be pecuniary. He who endeavours to enrich himself with the property of another, should be deprived of part of his own. But this crime, alas! is commonly the effect of misery and despair; the crime of that unhappy part of mankind, to whom the right of exclusive property (a terrible, and perhaps unnecessary right) has left but a bare existence. Besides, as pecuniary punishments may increase the number of robbers, by increasing the number of poor, and may deprive an innocent family of subsistence, the most proper punishment will be that kind of slavery, which alone can be called just; that is, which makes the society, for a

G 2   time.

time, abfolute mafter of the perfon, and
labour of the criminal, in order to oblige
him to repair, by this dependance, the
unjuft defpotifm he ufurped over the property of another, and his violation of the
focial compact.

WHEN robbery is attended with violence,
corporal punifhment fhould be added to
flavery. Many writers have fhewn the
evident diforder which muft arife from not
diftinguifhing the punifhment due to robbery with violence, and that due to theft
or robbery committed with dexterity, ab-
furdly making a fum of money equivalent
to a man's life. But it can never be fuperfluous to repeat again and again, thofe truths
of which mankind have not profited; for
political machines preferve their motion
much longer than others, and receive a new
impulfe with more difficulty. Thefe crimes
are in their nature abfolutely different, and
this axiom is as certain in politics, as in ma-
thematics, that between qualities of different natures, there can be no fimilitude.

CHAP.

CHAP. XXIII.

Of Infamy, confidered as a Punifhment.

THOSE injuries, which affect the
honour, that is, that juft portion of
efteem, which every citizen has a right
to expect from others, fhould be punifhed
with infamy. Infamy is a mark of the
public difapprobation, which deprives the
object of all confideration in the eyes of
his fellow citizens, of the confidence of
his country, and of that fraternity which
exifts between members of the fame fociety. This is not always in the power of the
laws. It is neceffary that the infamy inflicted by the laws fhould be the fame with
that which refults from the relations of
things, from univerfal morality, or from
that particular fyftem, adopted by the nation, and the laws, which governs the opinion of the vulgar. If, on the contrary,
one be different from the other, either the
laws will no longer be refpected, or the
received notions of morality and probity

G 3 will

will vanifh in fpight of the declamations of moralifts, which are always too weak to refift the force of example. If we declare thofe actions infamous, which are in themfelves indifferent, we leffen the infamy of thofe which are really infamous.

THE punifhment of infamy fhould not be too frequent, for the power of opinion grows weaker by repetition; nor fhould it be inflicted on a number of perfons at the fame time, for the infamy of many refolves itfelf into the infamy of none.

PAINFUL and corporal punifhments fhould never be applied to fanaticifm; for being founded on pride, it glories in perfecution. Infamy and ridicule only fhould be employed againft fanatics: if the firft, their pride will be over-balanced by the pride of the people; and we may judge of the power of the fecond, if we confider that even truth is obliged to fummon all her force, when attacked by error armed with ridicule. Thus by oppofing one paffion to another, and opinion to
opinion,

opinion, a wife legiflator puts an end to the admiration of the populace, occafioned by a falfe principle, the original abfurdity of which is veiled by fome well-deduced confequences.

THIS is the method to avoid confounding the immutable relations of things, or oppofing nature, whofe actions not being limited by time, but operating inceffantly, overturn and deftroy all thofe vain regulations, which contradict her laws. It is not only in the fine arts, that the imitation of nature is the fundamental principle; it is the fame in found policy, which is no other than the art of uniting, and directing to the fame end, the natural and immutable fentiments of mankind.

C H A P. XXIV.

Of Idlenefs.

A WISE government will not fuffer, in the midft of labour and induftry, that kind of political idlenefs, which is

con-

confounded, by rigid declaimers, with the leifure attending riches acquired by induftry, which is of ufe to an increafing fociety, when confined within proper limits. I call thofe politically idle, who neither contribute to the good of fociety by their labour, nor their riches; who continually accumulate, but never fpend; who are reverenced by the vulgar with ftupid admiration, and regarded by the wife with difdain; who, being victims to a monaftic life, and deprived of all incitement to that activity which is neceffary to preferve, or increafe its comforts, devote all their vigour to paffions of the ftrongeft kind, the paffions of opinion. I call not him idle, who enjoys the fruits of the virtues, or vices, of his anceftors, and in exchange for his pleafures, fupports the induftrious poor. It is not then the narrow virtue of auftere moralifts, but the laws, that fhould determine, what fpecies of idlenefs deferves punifhment.

CHAP.

C H A P. XXV.

Of Banishment, and Confiscation.

HE who disturbs the public tranquillity, who does not obey the laws, who violates the conditions on which men mutually support and defend each other, ought to be excluded from society, that is, banished.

IT seems, as if banishment should be the punishment of those, who being accused of an atrocious crime, are probably, but not certainly, guilty. For this purpose would be required a law, the least arbitrary, and the most precise possible; which should condemn to banishment, those who have reduced the community to the fatal alternative, either of fearing or punishing them unjustly; still, however, leaving them the sacred right of proving their innocence. The reasons ought to be stronger for banishing a citizen, than a stranger, a ftranger, and for the firft-accufation, than for one who hath been often accufed.[38]

SHOULD the perfon, who is excluded for ever from fociety, be deprived of his property? This queftion may be confidered in different lights. The confifcation of effects, added to banifhment, is a greater punifhment, than banifhment alone; there ought then to be fome cafes, in which, according to the crime, either the whole fortune fhould be confifcated, or part only, or none at all. The whole fhould be forfeited, when the law, which ordains banifhment, declares at the fame time, that all connexions, or relations, between the fociety and the criminal, are annihilated. In this cafe, the citizen dies; the man only remains, and with refpect to a political body, the death of the *citizen* fhould have the fame confequences with the death of the *man*. It feems to follow then, that in this cafe, the effects of the criminal fhould devolve to his lawful heirs. But it is not on account of this refinement that I difapprove of confifcations,

confifcations. If fome have infifted, that they were a reftraint to vengeance, and the violence of particulars, they have not reflected, that though punifhments be productive of good, they are not, on that account, more juft; to be juft, they muft be neceffary. Even an ufeful injuftice can never be allowed by a legiflator, who means to guard againft watchful tyranny; which, under the flattering pretext of momentary advantages, would eftablifh permanent principles of deftruction, and to procure the eafe of a few in a high ftation, would draw tears from thoufands of the poor.

THE law which ordains confifcations, fets a price on the head of the fubject, with the guilty punifhes the innocent, and by reducing them to indigence and defpair, tempts them to become criminal. Can there be a more melancholy fpectacle, than a whole family, overwhelmed with infamy and mifery, from the crime of their chief? a crime, which if it had been poffible, they were reftrained from preventing,

venting, by that fubmiffion which the laws themfelves have ordained.

C H A P. XXVI.

Of the Spirit of Family in States.

IT is remarkable, that many fatal acts of injuftice have been authorifed and approved, even by the wifeft and moft experienced men, in the freeft republics. This has been owing to their having confidered the ftate, rather as a fociety of *families*, than of *men*. Let us fuppofe a nation compofed of an hundred thoufand men, divided into twenty thoufand families of five perfons each, including the head or mafter of the family, its reprefentative. If it be an affociation of *families*, there will be twenty thoufand *men*, and eighty thoufand flaves; if of *men*, there will be an hundred thoufand citizens, and not one flave. In the firft cafe, we behold a republic, and twenty thoufand little monarchies, of which the heads are the

fovereigns;

fovereigns; in the fecond, the fpirit of
liberty will not only breathe in every public
place of the city, and in the affemblies of the
nation, but in private houfes, where men
find the greateft part of their happinefs or
mifery. As laws and cuftoms are always
the effect of the habitual fentiments of the
members of a republic, if the fociety be an
affociation of the heads of families, the fpirit of monarchy will gradually make its way
into the republic itfelf, as its effects will only
be reftrained by the oppofite interefts of
each, and not by an univerfal fpirit of liberty and equality. The private fpirit of
family is a fpirit of minutenefs, and confined to little concerns. Public fpirit, on
the contrary, is influenced by general principles, and from facts deduces general rules
of utility to the greateft number.

In a republic of families, the children
remain under the authority of the father,
as long as he lives, and are obliged to
wait until his death for an exiftence dependant on the laws alone. Accuftomed
to kneel and tremble in their tender years,
when

when their natural fentiments were lefs
reftrained by that caution, obtained by
experience, which is called moderation,
how fhould they refift thofe obftacles,
which vice always oppofes to virtué, in the
languor and decline of age, when the
defpair of reaping the fruits is alone
fufficient to damp the vigour of their re-
folutions?

In a republic, where every man is a
citizen, family fubordination is not the
effect of compulfion, but of contract; and
the fons difengaged from the natural
dependance, which the weaknefs of infancy
and the neceffity of education required,
become free members of fociety, but
remain fubject to the head of the family
for their own advantage, as in the grea
fociety.

In a republic of families, the young
people, that is the moft numerous, and
moft ufeful part of the nation, are at the
difcretion of their fathers: in a republic
of men, they are attached to their parents
by

by no other obligation, than that facred
and inviolable one of mutual affiftance,
and of gratitude for the benefits they
have received; a fentiment, deftroyed not
fo much by the wickednefs of the human
heart, as by a miftaken fubjection, pre-
fcribed by the laws.

THESE contradictions between the laws
of families, and the fundamental laws of
a ftate, are the fource of many others
between public and private morality, which
produce a perpetual conflict in the mind.
Domeftic morality infpires fubmiffion, and
fear: the other, courage and liberty. That
inftructs a man to confine his beneficence to
a fmall number of perfons, not of his own
choice; this, to extend it to all mankind;
that commands a continual facrifice of
himfelf to a vain idol, called the *good of the
family*, which is often no real good to any
one of thofe who compofe it; this teaches
him to confider his own advantage without
offending the laws, or excites him to facrifice
himfeif for the good of his country, by
rewarding him beforehand with the fanaticifm

ticifm it infpires. Such contradictions are the reafon, that men neglect the purfuit of virtue, which they can hardly diftinguifh midft the obfcurity and confufion of natural and moral objects. How frequently are men, upon a retrofpection of their actions, aftonifhed to find themfelves difhoneft?

In proportion to the increafe of fociety, each member becomes a fmaller part of the whole; and the republican fpirit diminifhes in the fame proportion, if neglected by the laws. Political focieties, like the human body, have their limits circumfcribed, which they cannot exceed without difturbing their œconomy. It feems as if the greatnefs of a ftate ought to be inverfely as the fenfibility and activity of the individuals; if on the contrary, population and activity increafe in the fame proportion, the laws will with difficulty prevent the crimes arifing from the good they have produced. An overgrown republic can only be faved from defpotifm, by fubdividing it into a number of confederate republics. But how is this practicable? By a

defpotic

despotic dictator, who, with the courage of *Sylla*,[39] has as much genius for building up, as that Roman had for pulling down. If he be an ambitious man, his reward will be immortal glory; if a philosopher, the blessings of his fellow-citizens will sufficiently console him for the loss of authority, though he should not be insensible to their ingratitude.

In proportion as the sentiments, which unite us to the state, grow weaker, those which attach us to the objects which more immediately surround us, grow stronger; therefore, in the most despotic government, friendships are more durable, and domestic virtues (which are always of the lowest class) are the most common, or the only virtues existing. Hence it appears how confined have been the views of the greatest number of legiflators.

C H A P.

CHAP. XXVII.

Of the Mildnefs of Punifhments.

THE courfe of my ideas has carried me away from my fubject, to the elucidation of which I now return. Crimes are more effectually prevented by the *certainty*, than the *feverity* of punifhment. Hence in a magiftrate, the neceffity of vigilance, and in a judge, of implacability, which, that it may become an ufeful virtue, fhould be joined to a mild legiflation. The certainty of a fmall punifhment will make a ftronger impreffion, than the fear of one more fevere, if attended with the hopes of efcaping; for it is the nature of mankind to be terrified at the approach of the fmalleft inevitable evil, whilft hope, the beft gift of heaven, hath the power of difpelling the apprehenfion of a greater; efpecially if fupported by examples of impunity, which weaknefs or avarice too frequently afford.

Ir

IF punishments be very severe, men are naturally led to the perpetration of other crimes, to avoid the punishment due to the first. The countries and times most notorious for severity of punishments, were always those in which the most bloody and inhuman actions and the most atrocious crimes were committed; for the hand of the legislator and the assassin were directed by the same spirit of ferocity; which, on the throne, dictated laws of iron to slaves and savages, and, in private, instigated the subject to sacrifice one tyrant to make room for another.

IN proportion as punishments become more cruel, the minds of men, as a fluid rises to the same height with that which surrounds it, grow hardened and insensible; and the force of the passions still continuing, in the space of an hundred years, the *wheel* terrifies no more than formerly the *prison*. That a punishment may produce the effect required, it is sufficient that the *evil* it occasions should exceed the *good* expected from the crime; including

H 2   in

in the calculation the certainty of the punifhment, and the privation of the expected advantage. All feverity beyond this is fu,erfluous, and therefore tyrannical.

MEN regulate there conduct by the repeated impreffion of evils they know, and not by thofe with which they are unacquainted. Let us, for example, fuppofe two nations, in one of which the greateft punifhment is *perpetual flavery*, and in the other *the wheel*. I fay, that both will infpire the fame degree of terror; and that there can be no reafons for increafing the punifhments of the firft; which are not equally valid for augmenting thofe of the fecond to more lafting and more ingenious modes of tormenting; and fo on to the moft exquifite refinements of a fcience too well known to tyrants.

THERE are yet two other confequences of cruel punifhments, which counter-act the purpofe of their inftitution, which was, to prevent crimes. The *firft* arifes

from

from the impoſſibility of eſtabliſhing an exact proportion between the crime and puniſhment, for though ingenious cruelty hath greatly multiplied the variety of torments, yet the human frame can ſuffer only to a certain degree, beyond which it is impoſſible to proceed, be the enormity of the crime ever ſo great, The *ſecond* conſequence is impunity. Human nature is limited no leſs in evil than in good. Exceſſive barbarity can never be more than temporary; it being impoſſible that it ſhould be ſupported by a permanent ſyſtem of legiſlation; for if the laws be too cruel they muſt be altered, or anarchy and impunity will ſucceed.

Is it poſſible, without ſhuddering with horror, to read in hiſtory of the barbarous and uſeleſs torments that were coolly invented and executed by men who were called ſages? Who does not tremble at the thoughts of thouſands of wretches, whom their miſery, either cauſed or tolerated by the laws, which favoured the few and outraged the many, had forced

H 3   in

in defpair to return to a ftate of nature; or accufed of impoffible crimes, the fabric of ignorance and fuperftition; or guilty only of having been faithful to their own principles; who, I fay, can, without horror, think of their being torn to pieces with flow and ftudied barbarity, by men endowed with the fame paffions and the fame feelings? A delightful fpectacle to a fanatic multitude!

C H A P. XXVIII.

Of the Punifhment of Death.

THE ufelefs profufion of punifhments, which has never made men better, induces me to enquire, whether the punifh-ment of *death* be really juft or ufeful in a well governed ftate? What *right*, I afk, have men to cut the throats of their fellow-creatures? Certainly not that on which the fovereignty and laws are founded. The laws, as I have faid before, are only the fum of the fmalleft portions of the

private

private liberty of each individual, and reprefent the general will, which is the aggregate of that of each individual. Did any one ever give to others the right of taking away his life? Is it poffible, that in the fmalleft portions of the liberty of each, facrificed to the good of the public, can be contained the greateft of all good, life? If it were fo, how fhall it be reconciled to the maxim which tells us, that a man has no right to kill himfelf? Which he certainly muft have, if he could give it away to another.

But the punifhment of death is not authorifed by any right; for I have demonftrated that no fuch right exifts. It is therefore a war of a whole nation againft a citizen, whofe deftruction they confider as neceffary, or ufeful to the general good. But if I can further demonftrate, that it is neither neceffary nor ufeful, I fhall have gained the caufe of humanity.

The death of a citizen cannot be neceffary, but in one cafe. When, though

H 4   deprived

deprived of his liberty, he has fuch power and connexions as may endanger the fecurity of the nation; when his exiftence may produce a dangerous revolution in the eftablifhed form of government. But even in this cafe, it can only be neceffary when a nation is on the verge of recovering or lofing its liberty; or in times of abfolute anarchy, when the diforders themfelves hold the place of laws. But in a reign of tranquillity; in a form of government approved by the united wifhes of the nation; in a ftate well fortified from enemies without, and fupported by ftrength within, and opinion, perhaps more efficacious; where all power is lodged in the hands of a true fovereign; where riches can purchafe pleafures and not authority, there can be no neceffity for taking away the life of a fubject.

If the experience of all ages be not fufficient to prove, that the punifhment of death has never prevented determined men from injuring fociety; if the example of the Romans; if twenty years reign of
Elizabeth,

Elizabeth, empreſs of Ruſſia, in which ſhe gave the fathers of their country an example more illuſtrious than many conqueſts bought with blood; if, I ſay, all this be not ſufficient to perſuade mankind, who always ſuſpect the voice of reaſon, and who chuſe rather to be led by authority, let us conſult human nature in proof of my aſſertion.

It is not the intenſeneſs of the pain that has the greateſt effect on the mind, but its continuance; for our ſenſibility is more eaſily and more powerfully affected by weak but repeated impreſſions, than by a violent, but momentary, impulſe. The power of habit is univerſal over every ſenſible being. As it is by that we learn to ſpeak, to walk, and to ſatisfy our neceſſities, ſo the ideas of morality are ſtamped on our minds by repeated impreſſions. The death of a criminal is a terrible but momentary ſpectacle, and therefore a leſs efficacious method of deterring others, than the continued example of a man deprived of his liberty, condemned, as a

beaſt

beaft of burthen, to repair, by his labour, the injury he has done to fociety. *If I commit fuch a crime*, fays the fpectator to himfelf, *I fhall be reduced to that miferable condition for the reft of my life.* A much more powerful preventive than the fear of death, which men always behold in diftant obfcurity.

THE terrors of death make fo flight an impreffion, that it has not force enough to withftand the forgetfulnefs natural to mankind, even in the moft effential things; efpecially when affifted by the paffions. Violent impreffions furprize us, but their effect is momentary; they are fit to produce thofe revolutions which inftantly transform a common man into a Lacede-monian or a Perfian; but in a free and quiet government they ought to be rather frequent than ftrong.

THE execution of a criminal is, to the multitude, a fpectacle, which in fome excites compaffion mixed with indig-nation. Thefe fentiments occupy the
mind

mind much more than that falutary terror which the laws endeavour to infpire; but in the contemplation of continued fuffering, terror is the only, or a leaft predominant fenfation. The feverity of a punifhment fhould be juft fufficient to excite compaffion in the fpectators, as it is intended more for them than for the criminal.

A PUNISHMENT, to be juft, fhould have only that degree of feverity which is fufficient to deter others. Now there is no man, who upon the leaft reflection, would put in competition the total and perpetual lofs of his liberty, with the greateft advantages he could poffibly obtain in confequence of a crime. Perpetual flavery, then, has in it all that is neceffary to deter the moft hardened and determined, as much as the punifhment of death. I fay it has more. There are many who can look upon death with intrepidity and firmnefs; fome through fanaticifm, and others through vanity, which attends us even to the grave; others

from

from a defperate refolution, either to get
rid of their mifery, or ceafe to live: but
fanaticifm and vanity forfake the criminal
in flavery, in chains and fetters, in an
iron cage; and defpair feems rather the
beginning than the end of their mifery.
The mind, by collecting itfelf and uniting
all its force, can, for a moment, repel
affailing grief; but its moft vigorous
efforts are infufficient to refift perpetual
wretchednefs.

In all nations, where death is ufed as
a punifhment, every example fuppofes a
new crime committed. Whereas in perpetual flavery, every criminal affords a
frequent and lafting example; and if it be
neceffary that men fhould often be witneffes of the power of the laws, criminals
fhould often be put to death; but this
fuppofes a frequency of crimes; and from
hence this punifhment will ceafe to have
its effect, fo that it muft be ufeful and ufelefs at the fame time.

I SHALL

I SHALL be told, that perpetual flavery is as painful a punifhment as death, and therefore as cruel. I anfwer, that if all the miferable moments in the life of a flave were collected into one point, it would be a more cruel punifhment than any other; but thefe are fcattered through his whole life, whilft the pain of death exerts all its force in a moment. There is alfo another advantage in the punifh-ment of flavery, which is, that it is more terrible to the fpectator than to the fuf-ferer himfelf; for the fpectator confiders the fum of all his wretched moments, whilft the fufferer, by the mifery of the prefent, is prevented from thinking of the future. All evils are increafed by the imagination, and the fufferer finds re-fources and confolations, of which the fpectators are ignorant; who judge by their own fenfibility of what paffes in a mind, by habit grown callous to misfor-tune.

LET us, for a moment, attend to the reafoning of a robber or affaffin, who is
deterred

deterred from violating the laws by the
gibbet or the wheel. I am fenfible, that
to develop the fentiments of one's own
heart, is an art which education only can
teach: but although a villain may not
be able to give a clear account of his
principles, they neverthelefs influence his
conduct. He reafons thus. " What are
" thefe laws, that I am bound to refpect,
" which make fo great a difference be-
" tween me and the rich man ? He re-
" fufes me the farthing I afk of him, and
" excufes himfelf, by bidding me have
" recourfe to labour with which he is
" unacquainted. Who made thefe laws?
" The rich and the great, who never
" deigned to vifit the miferable hut of
" the poor; who have never feen him
" dividing a piece of mouldly bread, amidft
" the cries of his famifhed children and
" the tears of his wife. Let us break thofe
" ties, fatal to the greateft part of man-
" kind, and only ufeful to a few indolent
" tyrants. Let us attack injuftice at its
" fource. I will return to my natural
" ftate of independance. I fhall live free
                                    " and

" and happy on the fruits of my courage
" and induſtry. A day of pain and re-
" pentance may come, but it will be
" ſhort; and for an hour of grief I ſhall
" enjoy years of pleaſure and liberty.
" King of a ſmall number, as determined
" as myſelf, I will correct the miſtakes
" of fortune; and I ſhall ſee thoſe tyrants
" grow pale and tremble at the ſight of
" him, whom, with inſulting pride, they
" would not ſuffer to rank with their dogs
" and horſes."

RELIGION then preſents itſelf to the
mind of this lawleſs villain, and promiſing
him almoſt a certainty of eternal happineſs
upon the eaſy terms of repentance, contributes much to leſſen the horror of the laſt
ſcene of the tragedy.

BUT he who foreſees, that he muſt paſs
a great number of years, even his whole
life, in pain and ſlavery; a ſlave to thoſe
laws by which he was protected; in ſight
of his fellow citizens, with whom he lives
in freedom and ſociety; makes an uſeful
comparifon

comparifon between thofe evils, the uncertainty of his fuccefs, and the fhortnefs of the time in which he fhall enjoy the fruits of his tranfgreffion. The example of thofe wretches continually before his eyes, makes a much greater impreffion on him than a punifhment, which, inftead of correcting, makes him more obdurate.

THE punifhment of death is pernicious to fociety, from the example of barbarity it affords. If the paffions, or the neceffity of war, have taught men to fhed the blood of their fellow creatures, the laws, which are intended to moderate the ferocity of mankind, fhould not increafe it by examples of barbarity, the more horrible, as this punifhment is ufually attended with formal pageantry. Is it not abfurd, that the laws, which deteft and punifh homicide, fhould, in order to prevent murder, publicly commit murder themfelves? What are the true and moft ufeful laws? Thofe compacts and conditions which all would propofe and obferve, in thofe moments when private intereft is filent, or combined

bined with that of the public. What are the natural fentiments of every perfon concerning the punifhment of death? We may read them in the contempt and indignation with which every one looks on the executioner, who is neverthelefs an innocent executor of the public will; a good citizen, who contributes to the advantage of fociety; the inftrument of the general fecurity within, as good foldiers are without. What then is the origin of this contradiction? Why is this fentiment of mankind indelible, to the fcandal of reafon? It is, that in a fecret corner of the mind, in which the original impreffions of nature are ftill preferved, men difcover a fentiment which tells them, that their lives are not lawfully in the power of any one, but of that neceffity only, which with its iron fcepter rules the univerfe.

WHAT muft men think, when they fee wife magiftrates and grave minifters of juftice, with indifference and tranquillity, dragging a criminal to death, and whilft a wretch trembles with agony, expecting

I   the

the fatal ſtroke, the judge, who has condemned him, with the coldeſt inſenſibility,
and perhaps with no ſmall gratification
from the exertion of his authority, quits
his tribunal to enjoy the comforts and
pleaſures of life? They will ſay, " Ah!
" thoſe cruel formalities of juſtice are
" a cloak to tyranny, they are a ſecret
" language, a ſolemn veil, intended to
" conceal the ſword by which we are ſacri-
" ficed to the inſatiable idol of deſpotiſm.
" Murder, which they would repreſent
" to us as an horrible crime, we ſee
" practiſed by them without repugnance,
" or remorſe. Let us follow their ex-
" ample. A violent death appeared ter-
" rible in their deſcriptions, but we ſee
" that it is the affair of a moment. It
" will be ſtill leſs terrible to him, who
" not expecting it, eſcapes almoſt all the
" pain." Such is the fatal, though ab-
ſurd reaſoning of men who are diſpoſed
to commit crimes; on whom, the abuſe
of religion has more influence than religion itſelf.

Iꜰ

IF it be objected, that almoſt all nations in all ages have puniſhed certain
crimes with death; I anſwer, that the
force of theſe examples vaniſhes, when
oppoſed to truth, againſt which preſcrip-
tion is urged in vain. The hiſtory of
mankind is an immenſe ſea of errors, in
which a few obſcure truths may here and
there be found.

BUT human ſacrifices have alſo been
common in almoſt all nations. That
ſome ſocieties only, either few in number,
or for a very ſhort time, abſtained from
the puniſhment of death, is rather favourable to my argument, for ſuch is the fate
of great truths, that their duration is only
as a flaſh of lightning in the long and dark
night of error. The happy time is not
yet arrived, when truth, as falſhood has
been hitherto, ſhall be the portion of the
greateſt number.

I AM ſenſible that the voice of one
philoſopher is too weak to be heard amidſt
the clamours of a multitude, blindly in-

I 2   fluenced

fluenced by cuftom; but there is a fmall
number of fages, fcattered on the face
of the earth, who will echo to me from
the bottom of their hearts; and if thefe
truths fhould haply force their way to
the thrones of princes, be it known to
them, that they come attended with the
fecret wifhes of all mankind; and tell
the fovereign who deigns them a gracious
reception, that his fame fhall outfhine
the glory of conquerors, and that equitable
pofterity will exalt his peaceful trophies
above thofe of a Titus, an Antoninus, or a
Trajan. [41]

How happy were mankind, if laws
were now to be firft formed; now that we
fee on the thrones of Europe, benevolent
monarchs, friends to the virtues of peace,
to the arts and fciences, fathers of their
people, though crowned yet citizens; the
increafe of whofe authority augments the
happinefs of their fubjects, by deftroying
that intermediate defpotifm, which inter-
cepts the prayers of the people, to the
throne.   If thefe humane princes have
                                    fuffered

ſuffered the old laws to ſubſiſt, it is doubt-
leſs becaüſe they are deterred by the num-
berleſs obſtacles, which oppoſe the ſub-
verſion of errors eſtabliſhed by the ſanction
of many ages; and therefore every wiſe citizen will wiſh for the increaſe of their
authority.

C H A P. XXIX.

Of Impriſonment.

THAT a magiſtrate, the executor of the
laws, ſhould have a power to impri-
ſon a citizen, to deprive the man he hates
of his liberty upon frivolous pretences,
and to leave his friend unpuniſhed, not-
withſtanding the ſtrongeſt proofs of his
guilt, is an error, as common, as it is contrary to the end of ſociety, which is perſo-
nal ſecurity.

IMPRISONMENT is a puniſhment, which
differs from all others in this particular,

I 3   that

that it neceſſarily precedes conviction; but this difference does not deſtroy a circumſtance, which is eſſential and common to it with all other puniſhments, *viz.* that it ſhould never be inflicted, but when ordained by the law. The law ſhould therefore determine the crime, the preſumption, and the evidence ſufficient to ſubject the accuſed to impriſonment and examination. Public report, his flight, his extrajudicial confeſſion, that of an accomplice, menaces, and his conſtant enmity with the perſon injured, the circumſtances of the crime, and ſuch other evidence, may be ſufficient to juſtify the impriſonment of a citizen. But the nature of this evidence ſhould be determined by the laws, and not by the magiſtrates, whoſe decrees are always contrary to political liberty, when they are not particular applications of a general maxim of the public code. When puniſhments become leſs ſevere, and priſons leſs horrible; when compaſſion and humanity ſhall penetrate the iron gates of dungeons, and direct the obdurate and inex-

inexorable minifters of juftice, the laws may then be fatisfied with weaker evidence for imprifonment.

A PERSON accufed, imprifoned, tried, and acquitted, ought not to be branded with any degree of infamy. Among the Romans, we fee that many, accufed of very great crimes and afterwards declared innocent, were refpected by the people, and honoured with employments in the ftate. But why is the fate of an innocent perfon fo different in this age? It is, becaufe the prefent fyftem of penal laws prefents to our minds an idea of power rather than of juftice. It is, becaufe the accufed and convicted are thrown indifcriminately into the fame prifon; becaufe imprifonment is rather a punifhment, than a means of fecuring the perfon of the accufed; and becaufe the interior power, which defends the laws, and the exterior, which defends the throne and kingdom, are feparate, when they fhould be united. If the firft were (under the common authority of the laws)

com-

combined with the right of judging, but not however immediately dependant on the magiſtrate, the pomp that attends a military corps, would take off the infamy; which, like all popular opinions, is more attached to the manner and form, than to the thing itſelf; as may be ſeen in military impriſonment, which, in the common opinion, is not ſo diſgraceful as the civil. But the barbarity and ferocity of our anceſtors, the hunters of the North, ſtill ſubſiſt among the people, in our cuſtoms and our laws, which are always ſeveral ages behind the actual refinements of a nation.

C H A P. XXX.

Of Proſecution and Preſcription.

THE proofs of the crime being obtained, and the certainty of it determined, it is neceſſary to allow the criminal time and means for his juſtification; but a time ſo ſhort, as not to diminiſh that promptitude of puniſhment, which, as we

have

have ſhewn, is one of the moſt powerful
means of preventing crimes. A miſtaken
humanity may objeᶜt to the ſhortneſs of
the time, but the force of the objeᶜtion
will vaniſh, if we conſider that the danger
of the innocent increaſes with the defeᶜts
of the legiſlation.

THE time for enquiry and for juſtification ſhould be fixed by the laws, and
not by the judge, who, in that caſe,
would become legiſlator. With regard
to atrocious crimes, which are long remembered, when they are once proved,
if the criminal have fled, no time ſhould
be allowed; but in leſs conſiderable and
more obſcure crimes, a time ſhould be
fixed, after which the delinquent ſhould be
no longer uncertain of his fate. For in the
latter caſe, the length of time, in which
the crime is almoſt forgotten, prevents the
example of impunity, and allows the criminal to amend, and become a better member of ſociety.

GENERAL

GENERAL principles will here be fufficient, it being impoffible to fix precifely
the limits of time for any given legiflation, or for any fociety in any particular
circumftance. I fhall only add, that in
a nation willing to prove the utility of
moderate punifhment, laws, which, according to the nature of the crime, increafe or diminifh the time of enquiry
and juftification, confidering the imprifonment or the voluntary exile of the
criminal as a part of the punifhment, will
form an eafy divifion of a fmall number
of mild punifhments for a great number of
crimes.

BUT, it muft be obferved, the time
for inquiry and juftification fhould not increafe in direct proportion to the atrocioufnefs of crimes; for the probability of
fuch crimes having been committed, is inverfely as their atrocioufnefs. Therefore
the time for inquiry, ought in fome cafes
to be diminifhed, and that for juftification
increafed, & *vice verfa*. This may appear

to

to contradict what I have said above, namely, that equal punifhments may be decreed
for unequal crimes, by confidering the
time allowed the criminal, or the prifon as
a punifhment.

In order to explain this idea, I fhall
divide crimes into two claffes. The firft
comprehends homicide, and all greater
crimes; the fecond, crimes of an inferior
degree. This diftinction is founded in
human nature. The prefervation of life
is a natural right; the prefervation of
property is a right of fociety. The motives that induce men to fhake off the
natural fentiment of compaffion, which
muft be deftroyed before great crimes can
be committed, are much lefs in number
than thofe, by which, from the natural
defire of being happy, they are inftigated
to violate a right, which is not founded
in the heart of man, but is the work of
fociety. The different degrees of probability in thefe two claffes, requires that
they fhould be regulated on different
principles. In the greateft crimes, as they
are

are less frequent, and the probability of the innocence of the accused being greater, the time allowed him for his justification should be greater, and the time of enquiry less. For by hastening the definitive sentence, the flattering hopes of impunity are destroyed, which are more dangerous, as the crime is more atrocious. On the contrary, in crimes of less importance, the probability of the innocence being less, the time of inquiry should be greater, and that of justification less, as impunity is not so dangerous.

But this division of crimes into two classes should not be admitted, if the consequences of impunity were in proportion to the probability of the crime. It should be considered, that a person accused, whose guilt or innocence is not determined for want of proofs, may be again imprisoned for the same crime, and be subject to a new trial, if fresh evidence arises, within the time fixed.

THIS

THIS is in my opinion the beſt method of providing, at the ſame time, for the ſecurity and liberty of the ſubject, without favouring one at the expence of the other; which may eaſily happen, ſince both theſe bleſſings, the inalienable and equal patrimony of every citizen, are liable to be invaded, the one by open or diſguiſed deſpotiſm, and the other by tumultuous and popular anarchy.

C H A P. XXXI.

Of Crimes of difficult Proof.

WITH the foregoing principles in view, it will appear aſtoniſhing, that reaſon hardly ever preſided at the formation of the laws of nations; that the weakeſt and moſt equivocal evidence, and even conjectures, have been thought ſufficient proof for crimes the moſt atrocious, (and therefore moſt improbable) the moſt obſcure and chimerical; as if it were the intereſt of the laws and the judge not to inquire

inquire into the truth, but to prove the crime; as if there were not a greater rifk of condemning an innocent perfon, when the probability of his guilt is lefs.

THE generality of men want that vigour of mind, and refolution, which are as neceffary for great crimes, as for great virtues; and which at the fame time produce both the one and the other in thofe nations, which are fupported by the activity of their government, and a paffion for the public good. For in thofe which fubfift by their greatnefs or power, or by the goodnefs of their laws, the paffions being in a weaker degree, feem calculated rather to maintain than to improve the form of government. This naturally leads us to an important conclufion, *viz.* that great crimes do not always produce the deftruction of a nation.

THERE are fome crimes, which, though frequent in fociety, are of difficult proof, a circumftance admitted, as equal to the probability of the innocence of the accufed.

But

But as the frequency of these crimes is not owing to their impunity, so much as to other causes, the danger of their passing unpunished is of less importance, and therefore the time of examination, and prescription, may be equally diminished. These principles are different from those commonly received; for it is in crimes, which are proved with the greatest difficulty, such as adultery, and sodomy, that presumptions, half-proofs, &c. are admitted; as if a man could be half innocent, and half guilty; that is, half punishable and half absolvable. It is in these cases that torture should exercise its cruel power on the person of the accused, the witnesses, and even his whole family, as, with unfeeling indifference, some Civilians have taught who pretend to dictate laws to nations.

ADULTERY is a crime, which, politically considered, owes its existence to two causes, viz. pernicious laws, and the powerful attraction between the sexes. This attraction is similar in many circumstances to gravity, the spring of motion in the

the univerfe. Like this, it is diminifhed by diftance; one regulates the motions of the body, the other of the foul. But they differ in one refpect; the force of gravity decreafes in proportion to the obftacles that oppofe it; the other gathers ftrength and vigour as the obftacles increafe.

IF I were fpeaking to nations guided only by the laws of nature, I would tell them, that there is a confiderable difference between adultery and all other crimes. Adultery proceeds from an abufe of that neceffity, which is conftant and univerfal in human nature; a neceffity anterior to the formation of fociety, and indeed the founder of fociety itfelf; whereas all other crimes tend to the deftruction of fociety, and arife from momentary paffions, and not from a natural neceffity. It is the opinion of thofe, who have ftudied hiftory and mankind, that this neceffity is conftantly in the fame degree in the fame climate. If this be true, ufelefs,

ufelefs, or rather pernicious muft all laws
and cuftoms be, which tend to diminifh the
fum total of the effects of this paffion.
Such laws would only burden one part of
fociety with the additional neceffities of
the other; but, on the contrary, wife are
the laws, which, following the natural
courfe of the river, divide the ftream into a
number of equal branches, preventing thus
both fterility and inundation.

CONJUGAL fidelity is always greater in
proportion as marriages are more numerous, and lefs difficult. But when the
intereft or pride of families, or paternal
authority, not the inclination of the parties, unite the fexes, gallantry foon breaks
the flender ties, in fpite of common moralifts, who exclaim againft the effect,
whilft they pardon the caufe. But thefe
reflections are ufelefs to thofe, who, living
in the true religion, act from fublimer
motives, which correct the eternal laws of
nature.

K   THE

THE act of adultery is a crime fo inftantaneous, fo myfterious, and fo concealed by the veil which the laws themfelves have woven; a veil neceffary indeed, but fo tranfparent, as to heighten rather than conceal the charms of the object; the opportunities are fo frequent, and the danger of difcovery fo eafily avoided, that it were much eafier for the laws to prevent this crime, than to punifh it when committed.

To every crime, which, from its nature muft frequently remain unpunifhed, the punifhment is an incentive. Such is the nature of the human mind, that difficulties, if not infurmountable, nor too great for our natural indolence, embellifh the object, and fpur us on to the purfuit. They are fo many barriers that confine the imagination to the object, and oblige us to confider it in every point of view. In this agitation, the mind naturally inclines and fixes itfelf to the moft agreeable part, ftudioufly avoiding every idea that might create difguft.

THE

THE crime of fodomy, fo feverely punifhed by the laws, and for the proof of
which are employed tortures, which often
triumph over innocence itfelf, has its
fource much lefs in the paffions of man
in a free and independant ftate, than in
fociety and a flave. It is much lefs the
effect of a fatiety in pleafures, than of that
education, which, in order to make men
ufeful to others, begins by making them
ufelefs to themfelves. In thofe public fe-
minaries, where ardent youth are carefully
excluded from all commerce with the other
fex, as the vigour of nature blooms, it is
confumed in a manner not only ufelefs to
mankind. but which accelerates the approach of old age.

THE murder of baftard-children is, in
like manner, the effect of a cruel dilemma,
in which a woman finds herfelf who has
been feduced through weaknefs, or overcome by force. The alternative is, either
her own infamy, or the death of a being,
who is incapable of feeling the lofs of
life. How can fhe avoid preferring the

K 2   laft

laſt to the inevitable miſery of herſelf and her unhappy infant? The beſt method of preventing this crime, would be effectually to protect the weak woman from that ty-ranny, which exaggerates all vices that cannot be concealed under the cloak of virtue.

I DO not pretend to leſſen that juſt ab-horrence which theſe crimes deſerve, but to diſcover the ſources from whence they ſpring; and I think I may draw the follow-ing concluſion: *That the puniſhment of a crime cannot be juſt, (that is neceſſary) if the laws have not endeavoured to prevent that crime by the beſt means which times and cir-cumſtances would allow.*

CHAP. XXXII.

Of Suicide.

SUICIDE is a crime which ſeems not to admit of puniſhment, properly ſpeaking; for it cannot be inflicted but on

the

the innocent, or upon an infenfible dead body. In the firft cafe, it is unjuft and tyrannical, for political liberty fuppofes all punifhments entirely perfonal; in the fecond, it has the fame effect, by way of example, as the fcourging a ftatue. Mankind love life too well; the objects that furround them; the feducing phantom of pleafure and hope, that fweeteft error of mortals, which makes men fwallow fuch large draughts of evil, mingled with a very few drops of good, allure them too ftrongly, to apprehend that this crime will ever be common from its unavoidable impunity. The laws are obeyed through fear of punifhment, but death deftroys all fenfibility. What motive then can reftrain the defperate hand of fuicide?

He who kills himfelf does a lefs injury to fociety, than he who quits his country for ever; for the other leaves his property behind him, but this carries with him at leaft a part of his fubftance. Befides, as the ftrength of a fociety confifts in the number of citizens, he who quits one na-

K 3   tion

tion to reside in another, becomes a double loss. This then is the question : whether it be advantageous to society, that its members should enjoy the unlimited privilege of migration ?

EVERY law that is not armed with force, or which, from circumstances, must be ineffectual, should not be promulgated. Opinion, which reigns over the minds of men, obeys the slow and indirect impressions of the legislator, but resists them when violently and directly applied ; and useless laws communicate their insignificance to the most salutary, which are regarded more as obstacles to be surmounted, than as safeguards of the public good. But further, our perceptions being limited, by inforcing the observance of laws which are evidently useless, we destroy the influence of the most salutary.

FROM this principle a wise dispenser of public happiness may draw some useful consequences, the explanation of which would carry me too far from my subject,
                                which

which is to prove the inutility of making
the nation a prifon.   Such a law is vain,
becaufe unlefs inacceffible rocks, or im-
paffable feas, divide the country from all
others, how will it be poffible to fecure
every point of the circumference, or how
will you guard the guards themfelves?
Befides, this crime once committed, cannot be punifhed; and to punifh it beforehand, would be to punifh the intention
and not the action; the will, which is
entirely out of the power of human laws.
To punifh the abfent by confifcating his
effects, befides the facility of collufion
which would inevitably be the cafe, and
which, without tyranny, could not be prevented, would put a ftop to all commerce
with other nations.   To punifh the criminal
when he returns, would be to prevent him
from repairing the evil he had already done
to fociety, by making his abfence perpetual.
Befides, any prohibition would increafe the
defire of removing, and would infallibly
prevent ftrangers from fettling in the
country.

WHAT

WHAT muſt we think of a government which has no means, but fear, to keep its ſubjects in their own country; to which, by the firſt impreſſions of their infancy, they are ſo ſtrongly attached.   The moſt certain method of keeping men at home, is, to make them happy; and it is the intereſt of every ſtate to turn the balance, not only of commerce, but of felicity in favour of its ſubjects.   The pleaſures of luxury are not the principal ſources of this happineſs; though, by preventing the too great accumulation of wealth in a few hands, they become a neceſſary remedy againſt the too great inequality of individuals, which always increaſes with the progreſs of ſociety. 47

WHEN the populouſneſs of a country does not increaſe in proportion to its extent, luxury favours deſpotiſm, for where men are moſt diſperſed, there is leaſt induſtry; and where there is leaſt induſtry, the dependance of the poor upon the luxury of the rich is greateſt, and the union of the oppreſſed againſt the oppreſſors is

leaſt

leaſt to be feared.   In ſuch circumſtances,
rich and powerful men more eaſily command diſtinction, reſpect and ſervice, by
which they are raiſed to a greater height
above the poor; for men are more independant the leſs they are obſerved, and are
leaſt obſerved when moſt numerous.   On
the contrary, when the number of people
is too great in proportion to the extent of
a country, luxury is a check to deſpotiſm;
becauſe it is a ſpur to induſtry, and becauſe the labour of the poor affords ſo many
pleaſures to the rich, that they diſregard the
luxury of oſtentation, which would remind
the people of their dependance.   Hence
we ſee, that in vaſt and depopulated ſtates,
the luxury of oſtentation prevails over that
of convenience; but in countries more po-
pulous, the luxury of convenience tends
conſtantly to diminiſh the luxury of oſtentation.

THE pleaſures of luxury have this inconvenience, that though they employ a
great number of hands, yet they are only
enjoyed by a few, whilſt the reſt, who do
not

not partake of them, feel the want more
fenfibly, on comparing their ftate with
that of others. Security and liberty, reftrained by the laws, are the bafis of happinefs, and when attended by thefe, the
pleafures of luxury favour population,
without which they become the inftru-
ments of tyranny. As the moft noble and
generous animals fly to folitude and inacceffible deferts, and abandon the fertile
plains to man, their greateft enemy; fo
men reject pleafure itfelf, when offered by
the hand of tyranny.

But to return. If it be demonftrated,
that the laws which imprifon men in their
own country are vain and unjuft, it will
be equally true of thofe which punifh
fuicide, for that can only be punifhed after
death; which is in the power of God
alone; but it is no crime, with regard to
man, becaufe the punifhment falls on an
innocent family. If it be objected, that
the confideration of fuch a punifhment
may prevent the crime; I anfwer, that
he who can calmly renounce the pleafure
of

of exiftence; who is fo weary of life, as to brave the idea of eternal mifery, will never be influenced by the more diftant, and lefs powerful confiderations of family, and children.

CHAP. XXXIII.

Of Smuggling.

SMUGGLING is a real offence againft the fovereign and the nation; but the punifhment fhould not brand the offender with infamy, becaufe this crime is not infamous in the public opinion. By inflicting infamous punifhments, for crimes that are not reputed fo, we deftroy that idea where it may be ufeful. If the fame punifhment be decreed for killing a pheafant as for killing a man, or for forgery, all difference between thofe crimes will fhortly vanifh. It is thus that moral fentiments are deftroyed in the heart of man; fentiments, the work of many ages and of much bloodfhed; fentiments that are

fo

fo flowly, and with fo much difficulty produced, and for the eftablifhment of which fuch fublime motives, and fuch an apparatus of ceremonies were thought neceffary.

THIS crime is owing to the laws themfelves; for the higher the duties, the greater is the advantage, and confequently, the temptation; which temptation is increafed by the facility of perpetration, when the circumference that is guarded is of great extent, and the merchandife prohibited is fmall in bulk. The feizure and lofs of the goods attempted to be fmuggled, together with thofe that are found along with them, is juft; but it would be better to leffen the duty, becaufe men rifque only in proportion to the advantage expected.

THIS crime being a theft of what belongs to the prince, and confequently, to the nation, why is it not attended with infamy? I anfwer, that crimes, which men confider as productive of no bad confequences

fequences to themfelves, do not intereſt
them fufficiently to excite their indignation.   The generality of mankind, upon
whom remote confequences make no im-
preſſion, do not fee the evil that may refult from the practice of fmuggling, efpecially if they reap from it any prefent advantage.   They only perceive the lofs fuf-
tained by the prince.   They are not then
intereſted in refuſing their eſteem to the
fmuggler, as to one who has committed
a theft or a forgery, or other crimes, by
which they themfelves may fuffer; from
this evident principle, that a fenſible being
only intereſts himfelf in thofe evils, with
which he is acquainted.

SHALL this crime then, committed by
one who has nothing to lofe, go unpuniſhed? No.   There are certain fpecies of
fmuggling, which fo particularly affect the
revenue, a part of government fo eſſential,
and managed with fo much difficulty, that
they deferve imprifonment, or even flavery;
but yet of fuch a nature as to be proportioned

tioned to the crime. For example, it would be highly unjuft that a fmuggler of tobacco fhould fuffer the fame punifhment with a robber, or affaffin; but it would be moft conformable to the nature of the offence, that the produce of his labour fhould be applied to the ufe of the crown, which he intended to defraud.

CHAP. XXXIV.

Of Bankrupts.

THE neceffity of good faith in contracts, and the fupport of commerce, oblige the legiflature to fecure, for the creditors, the perfons of bankrupts. It is, however, neceffary to diftinguifh between the fraudulent and the honeft bankrupt. The fraudulent bankrupt fhould be punifhed in the fame manner with him who adulterates the coin; for to falfify a piece of coin, which is a pledge of the mutual obligations between citizens, is not a greater crime

crime than to violate the obligations themfelves. But the bankrupt who, after a
ftrict examination, has proved before proper judges, that either the fraud, or loffes
of others, or misfortunes unavoidable by
human prudence, have ftript him of his
fubftance; upon what barbarous pretence
is he thrown into prifon, and thus deprived
of the only remaining good, the melancholy enjoyment of mere liberty? Why is
he ranked with criminals, and in defpair
compelled to repent of his honefty? Con-
fcious of his innocence, he lived eafy and
happy under the protection of thofe laws,
which, it is true, he violated but not inten-
tionally. Laws, dictated by the avarice of
the rich, and accepted by the poor, feduced
by that univerfal and flattering hope which
makes men believe, that all unlucky acci-
dents are the lot of others, and the moft
fortunate only their fhare. Mankind,
when influenced by the firft impreffions,
love cruel laws, although, being fubject to
them themfelves, it is the intereft of every
perfon that they fhould be as mild as poffible; but the fear of being injured is always

ways more prevalent than the intention of injuring others.

But to return to the honeſt bankrupt. Let his debt, if you will, not be conſidered as cancelled, 'till the payment of the whole; let him be refuſed the liberty of leaving the country without leave of his creditors, or of carrying into another nation that induſtry, which, under a penalty, he ſhould be obliged to employ for their benefit; but what pretence can juſtify the depriving an innocent, though unfortunate man of his liberty, without the leaſt utility to his creditors?

But ſay they, the hardſhips of confinement will induce him to diſcover his fraudulent tranſactions; an event, that can hardly be ſuppoſed, after a rigorous examination of his conduct and affairs. But if they are not diſcovered, he will eſcape unpuniſhed. It is, I think, a maxim of government, that the importance of the political inconveniences, ariſing from the impunity of a crime, are
directly

directly as the injury to the publick, and inverfely as the difficulty of proof.

IT will be neceffary to diftinguifh fraud attended with aggravating circumftances from fimple fraud, and that from perfect innocence. For the firft, let there be ordained the fame punifhment. as for forgery; for the fecond, a lefs punifhment, but with the lofs of liberty; and if perfectly honeft, let the bankrupt himfelf chufe the method of re-eftablifhing himfelf and of fatisfying his creditors; or if he fhould appear not to have been ftrictly honeft, let that be determined by his creditors. But thefe diftinctions fhould be fixed by the laws, which alone are impartial, and not by the arbitrary and dangerous prudence of Judges.*

WITH

* It may be alledged, that the intereft of commerce and property fhould be fecured; but commerce and property are not the end of the focial compact, but the means of obtaining that end; and to expofe all the members of fociety to cruel laws, to preferve them from evils, neceffarily occafioned by the infinite combinations which refult from the actual ftate of political

L   focieties,

WITH what eafe might a fagacious legiſlator prevent the greateſt part of fraudulent bankruptcies, and remedy the misfortunes that befall the honeſt and induſ-
trious! A public regiſter of all contracts,
with the liberty of confulting it allowed
to every citizen; a public fund formed by
a contribution of the opulent merchants
for the timely affiſtance of unfortunate induſtry, were eſtabliſhments that could produce no real inconveniences, and many advantages. But unhappily, the moſt fimple,
the eaſieſt, yet the wifeſt laws, that wait
only for the nod of the legiſlator, to dif-
fuſe through nations, wealth, power, and
felicity; laws, which would be regarded

focieties, would be to make the end fubfervient to the
means, a paralogiſm in all fciences, and particularly in
politicks. In the former editions of this work, I myſelf
fell into this error, when I faid that the honeſt bankrupt ſhould be kept in cuſtody, as a pledge for his debts,
or employed, as a flave, to work for his creditors. I am
aſhamed of having adopted fo cruel an opinion. I have
been accuſed of impiety; I did not deferve it. I have
been accuſed of fedition; I deferved it as little. But I
infulted all the rights of humanity, and was never re-
proached.

by

by future generations with eternal gratitude, are either unknown, or rejected. A
reftlefs, and trifling fpirit, the timid prudence of the prefent moment, a diftruft
and averfion to the moft ufeful novelties,
poffefs the minds of thofe who are im-
powered to regulate the actions of mankind.

C H A P. XXXV.

Of Sanctuaries.

ARE fanctuaries juft? Is a convention
between nations mutually to give
up their criminals, ufeful?

In the whole extent of a political ftate,
there fhould be no place independent of the
laws. Their power fhould follow every
fubject, as the fhadow follows the body.
Sanctuaries and impunity differ only in degree, and as the effect of punifhments depends more on their certainty, than their
greatnefs, men are more ftrongly invited

to crimes by fanctuaries, than they are deterred by punifhment. To increafe the
number of fanctuaries, is to erect fo many
little fovereignties; for, where the laws
have no power, new bodies will be formed in oppofition to the public good, and a
fpirit eftablifhed contrary to that of the
ftate. Hiftory informs us, that from the ufe
of fanctuaries have arifen the greateft revolutions in kingdoms, and in opinions.

SOME have pretended, that in whatever
country a crime, that is an action contrary
to the laws of fociety, be committed, the
criminal may be juftly punifhed for it in
any other: as if the character of fubject
were indelible, or fynonimous with, or
worfe than that of flave; as if a man could
live in one country, and be fubject to the
laws of another, or be accountable for his
actions to two fovereigns, or two codes of
laws, often contradictory. There are alfo
who think, that an act of cruelty committed, for example, at Conftantinople,
may be punifhed at Paris; for this ab-
ftracted reafon, that he who offends humanity,

manity, fhould have enemies in all mankind, and be the object of univerfal execration; as if judges were to be the knights errant of human nature in general, rather than guardians of particular conventions between men. The place of punifhment can certainly be no other, than that where the crime was committed; for the neceffity of punifhing an individual for the general good fubfifts there, and there only. A villain, if he has not broke through the conventions of a fociety, of which by my fuppofition he was not a member, may be feared, and by force banifhed and excluded from that fociety; but ought not to be formally punifhed by the laws, which were only intended to maintain the focial compact, and not to punifh the intrinfick malignity of actions.

WHETHER it be ufeful that nations fhould mutually deliver up their criminals? Although the certainty of there being no part of the earth where crimes are not punifhed, may be a means of preventing them, I fhall not pretend to determine this

L 3   queftion,

queſtion, until laws more conformable to
the neceſſities and rights of humanity, and
until milder puniſhments, and the aboli-
tion of the arbitrary power of opinion, ſhall
afford ſecurity to virtue and innocence
when oppreſſed; and until tyranny ſhall
be confined to the plains of Aſia, and Europe acknowledge the univerſal empire of
reaſon, by which the intereſts of ſovereigns,
and ſubjeɡts, are beſt united.

CHAP. XXXVI.

Of Rewards for apprehending, or killing Criminals.

LET us now inquire, whether it be
advantageous to ſociety, to ſet a price
on the head of a crimiral, and ſo to make
of every citizen an executioner. If the offender hath taken refuge in another ſtate,
the ſovereign encourages his ſubjeɡts to
commit a crime, and to expoſe themſelves
to a juſt puniſhment; he inſults that nation

tion, and authorizes the subjects to commit on their neighbours similar usurpations. If the criminal still remain in his own country, to set a price upon his head, is the strongest proof of the weakness of the government. He who has strength to defend himself, will not purchase the assistance of another. Besides such an edict confounds all the ideas of virtue, and morality, already too wavering in the mind of man. At one time treachery is punished by the laws, at another encouraged. With one hand the legislature strengthens the ties of kindred, and friendship, and with the other, rewards the violation of both. Always in contradiction with himself, now he invites the suspecting minds of men to mutual confidence, and now he plants distrust in every heart. To prevent one crime, he gives birth to a thousand. Such are the expedients of weak nations, whose laws are like temporary repairs to a tottering fabrick. On the contrary, as a nation becomes more enlightened, honesty and mutual confidence become more necessary,

L 4   and

and are daily tending to unite with found policy. Artifice, cabal, and obfcure and indirect actions are more eafily difcovered, and the intereft of the whole is better fecured againft the paffions of the individual.

EVEN the times of ignorance, when private virtue was encouraged by publick morality, may afford inftruction and example to more enlightened ages. But laws, which reward treafon, exite clandeftine war, and mutual diftruft, and oppofe that neceffary union of morality and policy, which is the foundation of happinefs, and univerfal peace.

C H A P. XXXVII.

Of Attempts, Accomplices, and Pardon.

THE laws do not punifh the intention; neverthelefs, an attempt, which manifefts the intention of committing a crime, deferves a punifhment; though lefs, perhaps, than if the crime were actually perpetrated.

petrated. The importance of preventing even attempts to commit a crime sufficiently authorifes a punifhment; but as there may be an interval of time between the attempt and the execution, it is proper to referve the greater punifhment for the actual commiffion, that even after the attempt there may be a motive for defifting.

In like manner, with regard to the accomplices, they ought not to fuffer fo fevere a punifhment as the immediate perpetrator of the crime. But this for a different reafon. When a number of men unite, and run a common rifk, the greater the danger, the more they endeavour to diftribute it equally. Now, if the principals be punifhed more feverely than the acceffaries, it will prevent the danger from being equally divided, and will increafe the difficulty of finding a perfon to execute the crime, as his danger is greater by the difference of the punifhment. There can be but one exception to this rule; and that is, when the principal receives

a reward

a reward from the accomplices. In that
cafe, as the difference of the danger is com-
penfated, the punifhment fhould be equal.
Thefe reflections may appear too refined
to thofe who do not confider, that it is of
great importance, that the laws fhould
leave the affociates as few means as poffible
of agreeing among themfelves.

In fome tribunals a pardon is offered
to an accomplice in a great crime, if he
difcover his affociates.   This expedient
has its advantages and difadvantages.   The
difadvantages are, that the law authorifes
treachery, which is detefted even by the
villains themfelves; and introduces crimes
of cowardice, which are much more pernicious to a nation than crimes of courage.
Courage is not common, and only wants
a benevolent power to direct it to the public good.   Cowardice, on the contrary,
is a frequent, felf-interefted and conta-
gious evil, which can never be improved
into a virtue.   Befides, the tribunal, which
has recourfe to this method, betrays its
fallibility, and the laws their weaknefs,

by

by imploring the affiftance of thofe by whom they are violated.

THE advantages are, that it prevents great crimes, the effects of which being public, and the perpetrators concealed, terrify the people. It alfo contributes to prove, that he who violates the laws, which are public conventions, will alfo violate private compacts. It appears to me, that a general law, promifing a reward to every accomplice who difcovers his affociates, would be better than a fpecial declaration in every particular cafe; becaufe it would prevent the union of thofe villains, as it would infpire a mutual diftruft, and each would be afraid of expofing himfelf alone to danger. The accomplice, however, fhould be pardoned, on condition of tranfportation. . . . . . But it is in vain, that I torment myfelf with endeavouring to extinguifh the remorfe I feel in attempting to induce the facred laws, the monument of publick confidence, the foundation of human morality, to authorife diffimulation and perfidy.

fidy. But what an example does it offer
to a nation, to fee the interpreters of the
laws break their promife of pardon, and
on the ftrength of learned fubtleties, and
to the fcandal of public faith, drag him to
punifhment who hath accepted of their
invitation! Such examples are not uncommon, and this is the reafon, that political fociety is regarded as a complex
machine, the fprings of which are moved
at pleafure by the moft dextrous or moft
powerful.

CHAP. XXXVIII.

Of Suggeftive Interrogations.

THE laws forbid *suggeftive interrogations*; that is, according to the civilians, queftions, which, with regard to the
circumftances of the crime, are *fpecial* when
they fhould be *general*; or, in other words,
thofe queftions, which having an immediate reference to the crime, fuggeft to
the criminal an immediate anfwer. Interrogations,

terrogations, according to the law, ought
to lead to the fact indirectly and oblique-
ly, but never directly or immediately.
The intent of this injunction is either,
that they should not suggest to the accused
an immediate answer that might acquit
him, or that they think it contrary to nature that a man should accuse himself.
But whatever be the motive, the laws
have fallen into a palpable contradiction,
in condemning suggestive interrogations,
whilst they authorise torture. Can there
be an interrogation more suggestive than
pain? Torture will suggest to a robust
villain an obstinate silence, that he may
exchange a greater punishment for a less;
and to a feeble man confession, to relieve
him from the present pain, which affects
him more than the apprehension of the
future. If a special interrogation be contrary to the right of nature, as it obliges
a man to accuse himself, torture will certainly do it more effectually. But men are
influenced more by the names than the nature of things.

HE,

HE, who obftinately refufes to anfwer the interrogatories, deferves a punifhment, which fhould be fixed by the laws, and that of the fevereft kind; that criminals fhould not, by their filence, evade the example which they owe the public. But this punifhment is not neceffary when the guilt of the criminal is indifputabie, becaufe in that cafe interrogation is ufelefs, as is likewife his confeffion, when there are, without it, proofs fufficient. This laft cafe is moft common, for experience fhews, that in the greateft number of criminal profecutions, the culprit pleads not guilty.

CHAP. XXXIX.

Of a particular Kind of Crimes.

THE reader will perceive, that I have omitted fpeaking of a certain clafs of crimes which has covered Europe with blood, and raifed up thofe horrid piles,

from

from whence, midst clouds of whirling
smoke, the groans of human victims, the
crackling of their bones, and the frying of
their still panting bowels, were a pleasing
spectacle, and agreeable harmony to the
fanatic multitude. But men of understanding will perceive, that the age and
country, in which I live, will not permit
me to inquire into the nature of this
crime.[49] It were too tedious, and foreign
to my subject, to prove the necessity of a
perfect uniformity of opinions, in a state,
contrary to the examples of many nations;
to prove that opinions, which differ from
one another only in some subtile and obscure distinctions, beyond the reach of human capacity, may nevertheless disturb the
public tranquillity, unless one only religion be established by authority; and that
some opinions, by being contrasted and
opposed to each other, in their collision
strike out the truth; whilst others, feeble
in themselves, require the support of
power and authority. It would, I say,
carry me too far, were I to prove, that
how odious soever is the empire of force
over

over the opinions of mankind, from whom
it only obtains diffimulation, followed by
contempt; and, although it may feem
contrary to the fpirit of humanity and
brotherly love, commanded us by reafon,
and authority, which we more refpect, it
is neverthelefs neceffary and indifpenfible.
We are to believe, that all thefe para-
doxes are folved beyond a doubt, and are
conformable to the true interefts of mankind, if practifed by a lawful authority.
I write only of *crimes* which violate the
laws of nature and the focial contract, and
not of *fins*, even the temporal punifhments
of which muft be determined from other
principles, than thofe of limited human
philofophy.

C H A P. XL.

Of falfe Ideas of Utility.

A PRINCIPAL fource of errors and injuftice, are falfe ideas of utility. For
example; that legiflator has falfe ideas of
utility,

utility, who confiders particular more than general conveniences; who had rather command the fentiments of mankind, than excite them, and dares fay to reafon, "Be thou a flave;" who would facrifice a thoufand real advantages, to the fear of an imaginary or trifling inconvenience; who would deprive men of the ufe of fire, for fear of their being burnt, and of water, for fear of their being drowned; and who knows of no means of preventing evil but by deftroying it.

THE laws of this nature, are thofe which forbid to wear arms, difarming thofe only who are not difpofed to commit the crime which the laws mean to prevent. Can it be fuppofed, that thofe who have the courage to violate the moft facred laws of humanity, and the moft important of the code, will refpect the lefs confiderable and arbitrary injunctions, the violation of which is fo eafy, and of fo little comparative importance? Does not the execution of this law deprive the fubject of that perfonal liberty, fo dear to mankind and to

M   the

the wife legiflator ; and does it not fubject
the innocent to all the difagreeable circumftances that fhould only fall on the guilty ?
It certainly makes the fituation of the af-
faulted worfe, and of the affailants better,
and rather encourages than prevents murder, as it requires lefs courage to attack
armed than unarmed perfons.

It is a falfe idea of utility, that would
give to a multitude of fenfible beings, that
fymmetry and order, which inanimate
matter is alone capable of receiving ; to
neglect the prefent, which are the only
motives that act with force and conftancy
on the multitude, for the more diftant,
whofe impreffions are weak and tranfitory,
unlefs increafed by that ftrength of imagination, fo very uncommon among mankind.   Finally, that it is a falfe idea of utility, which, facrificing things to names,
feparates the public good from that of individuals.

There is this difference between a
ftate of fociety and a ftate of nature, that
a favage

a favage does no more mifchief to another than is neceffary to procure fome benefit to himfelf; but a man in fociety is fometimes tempted, from a fault in the laws, to injure another, without any profpect of advantage. The tyrant infpires his vaffals with fear and fervility, which rebound upon him with double force, and are the caufe of his torment. Fear, the more private and domeftic it is, the lefs dangerous is it to him who makes it the inftrument of his happinefs; but the more it is public, and the greater number of people it affects, the greater is the probability that fome mad, defperate, or defigning perfon will feduce others to his party, by flattering expectations; and this will be the more eafily accomplifhed, as the danger of the enterprize will be divided amongft a greater number, becaufe the value the unhappy fet upon their exiftence is lefs, as their mifery is greater.

CHAP.

C H A P. XLI.

Of the Means of preventing Crimes.

IT is better to prevent crimes, than to
   punish them.   This is the fundamental principle of good legislation, which is
the art of conducting men to the *maximum*
of happiness, and to the *minimum* of misery,
if we may apply this mathematical expref-
fion to the good and evil of life.   But the
means hitherto employed for that purpose, are generally inadequate, or contrary to the end proposed.   It is impossible to reduce the tumultuous activity of
mankind to absolute regularity ; for, midst
the various and opposite attractions of
pleasure and pain, human laws are not
sufficient entirely to prevent disorders in
society.   Such however is the chimera
of weak men, when invested with authority.   To prohibit a number of indifferent actions, is not to prevent the crimes
which they may produce, but to create
                                           new

new ones; it is to change at will the ideas
of virtue and vice, which, at other times,
we are told are eternal and immutable.
To what a fituation fhould we be reduced,
if every thing were to be forbidden that
might poffibly lead to a crime? We muft
be deprived of the ufe of our fenfes. For
one motive that induces a man to commit
a real crime, there are a thoufand which
excite him to thofe indifferent actions,
which are called crimes by bad laws. If,
then, the probability that a crime will be
committed, be in proportion to the number of motives, to extend the fphere of
crimes will be to increafe that probability.
The generality of laws are only exclufive
privileges; the tribute of all to the advantage of a few.

WOULD you prevent crimes? Let the
laws be clear and fimple; let the entire
force of the nation be united in their defence; let them be intended rather to favour every individual, than any particulár
claffes of men; let the laws be feared,
and the laws only. The fear of the laws

is

is falutary, but the fear of men is a fruitful and fatal fource of crimes. Men en-
flaved, are more voluptuous, more de-
bauched, and more cruel than thofe who
are in a ftate of freedom. Thefe ftudy
the fciences, the intereft of nations, have
great objects before their eyes, and imitate them; but thofe, whofe views are
confined to the prefent moment, endeavour,
'midft the diftraction of riot. and debauche-
ry, to forget their fituation; accuftomed
to the uncertainty of all events, for the
laws determine none, the confequences of
their crimes become problematical, which
gives an additional force to the ftrength of
their paffions.

In a nation, indolent from the nature
of the climate, the uncertainty of the laws
confirms and increafes men's indolence and
ftupidity.   In a voluptuous, but active nation, this uncertainty occafions a multipli-
city of cabals and intrigues, which fpread
diftruft and diffidence through the hearts of
all, and diffimulation and treachery are the
foundation of their prudence.   In a brave
                                                and

and powerful nation, this uncertainty of the laws is at laft deftroyed, after many ofcillations from liberty to flavery, and from flavery to liberty again.

C H A P. XLII.

Of the Sciences.

WOULD you prevent crimes? Let liberty be attended with knowledge. As knowledge extends, the difadvantages which attend it diminifh, and the advantages increafe. A daring impoftor, who is always a man of fome genius, is adored by the ignorant populace, and defpifed by men of underftanding. Knowledge facilitates the comparifon of objects, by fhewing them in different points of view. When the clouds of ignorance are difpelled by the radiance of knowledge, authority trembles, but the force of the laws remains immoveable. Men of enlightened underftanding muft neceffarily approve thofe ufeful conventions, which are the foundation

M 4   of

of public fafety; they compare, with the higheft fatisfaction, the inconfiderable portion of liberty of which they are deprived, with the fum total facrificed by others for their fecurity; obferving that they have only given up the pernicious liberty of injuring their fellow creatures, they blefs the throne, and the laws upon which it is eftablifhed.

It is falfe that the fciences have always been prejudicial to mankind. When they were fo, the evil was inevitable. The multiplication of the human fpecies on the face of the earth introduced war, the rudiments of arts, and the firft laws, which were temporary compacts arifing from neceffity, and perifhing with it. This was the firft philofophy, and its few elements were juft, as indolence and want of fagacity, in the early inhabitants of the world, preferved them from error.

But neceffities increafing with the number of mankind, ftronger and more lafting impreffions were neceffary to prevent their

frequent

frequent relapfes into a ftate of barbarity, which became every day more fatal. The firft religious errors, ·which peopled the earth with falfe divinities, and created a world of invifible béings to govern the vifible creation, were of the utmoft fervice to mankind. The greateft benefactors to humanity were thofe who dared to deceive, and lead pliant ignorance to the foot of the altar. By prefenting to the minds of the vulgar, things out of the reach of their fenfes, which fled as they purfued, and always eluded their grafp; which, as they never comprehended, they never defpifed, their different paffions were united, and attached to a fingle object.[50] This was the firft tranfition of all nations from their favage ftate. Such was the neceffary, and perhaps the only bond of all focieties at their firft formation. I fpeak not of the chofen people of God, to whom the moft extraordinary miracles, and the moft fignal favours, fupplied the place of human policy. But as it is the nature of error to fub-divide itfelf *ad infinitum*, fo the pretended knowledge, which fprung from it, transformed mankind

kind into a blind fanatic multitude, jarring
and deftroying each other in the labyrinth
in which they were inclofed : hence it is
not wonderful, that fome fenfible and phi-
lofophic minds fhould regret the ancient
ftate of barbarity.   This was the firft epocha, in which knowledge, or rather opinions, were fatal. [51]

THE fecond may be found in the difficult and terrible paffage from error to truth,
from darknefs to light.   The violent fhock
between a mafs of errors, ufeful to the few
and powerful, and the truths fo important
to the many and the weak, with the fermentation of paffions, excited on that occafion, were productive of infinite evils to
unhappy mortals.   In the ftudy of hiftory,
whofe principal periods, after certain inter-
vals, much refemble each other, we frequently find, in the neceffary paffage from
the obfcurity of ignorance to the light of
philofophy, and from tyranny to liberty,
its natural confequence, one generation facrificed to the happinefs of the next. [52] But
when this flame is extinguifhed, and the
world

world delivered from its evils, truth, after a very flow progrefs, fits down with monarchs on the throne, and is worfhipped in the affemblies of nations. Shall we then believe, that light diffufed among the people is more deftructive than darknefs, and that the knowledge of the relations of things can ever be fatal to mankind ?

IGNORANCE may indeed be lefs fatal than a fmall degree of knowledge, becaufe this adds, to the evils of ignorance, the inevitable errors of a confined view of things on this fide the bounds of truth; but a man of enlightened underftanding, appointed guardian of the laws, is the greateft bleffing that a fovereign can beftow on a nation. Such a man is accuftomed to behold truth, and not to fear it; unacquainted with the greateft part of thofe imaginary and infatiable neceffities, which fo often put virtue to the proof, and accuftomed to contemplate mankind from the moft elevated point of view, he confiders the nation as his family, and his fellow citizens as brothers; the diftance between
the

the great and the vulgar appears to him the
lefs, as the number of mankind he has in
view is greater.

THE philofopher has neceffities and interefts unknown to the vulgar, and the
chief of thefe is not to belie in public the
principles he taught in obfcurity, and the
habit of loving virtue for its own fake.
A few fuch philofophers would conftitute
the happinefs of a nation; which, however, would be but of fhort durarion, unlefs by good laws, the number were fo increafed, as to leffen the probability of an
improper choice.

C H A P. XLIII.

Of Magiftrates.

ANOTHER method of preventing
crimes is, to make the obfervance of
the laws, and not their violation, the intereft of the magiftrate.

THE

THE greater the number of thofe who conftitute the tribunal, the lefs is the danger of corruption; becaufe the attempt will be more difficult, and the power and temptation of each individual will be proportionably lefs. If the fovereign, by pomp and the aufterity of edicts, and by refufing to hear the complaints of the oppreffed, accuftom his fubjects to refpect the magiftrates more than the laws, the magiftrates will gain indeed, but it will be at the expence of public and private fecurity.

C H A P.   XLIV.

Of Rewards.

YET another method of preventing crimes is, to reward virtue. Upon this fubject the laws of all nations are filent. If the rewards, propofed by academies for the difcovery of ufeful truths, have increafed our knowledge, and multiplied good books, is it not probable, that re-
.wards,

wards, diftributed by the beneficent hand
of a fovereign, would alfo multiply virtuous actions. The coin of honour is in-
exhauftible, and is abundantly fruitful in
the hands of a prince who diftributes it
wifely.

CHAP. XLV.

Of Education.

FINALLY, the moft certain method of -
preventing crimes is, to perfect the fyftem of education. But this is an object too
vaft, and exceeds my plan; an object, if
I may venture to declare it, which is fo inti-
mately connected with the nature of government, that it will always remain a barren
fpot, cultivated only by a few wife men.

A GREAT man, who is perfecuted by
that world he hath enlightened, and to
whom we are indebted for many important truths, hath moft amply detailed the
principal maxims of ufeful education.
                                    This

This chiefly confifts in prefenting to the mind a fmall number of felect objects; in fubftituting the originals for the copies, both of phyfical and moral phænomena; in leading the pupil to virtue by the eafy road of fentiment, and in withholding him from evil by the infallible power of necef-fary inconveniences, rather than by com-mand, which only obtains a counterfeit and momentary obedience.

CHAP. XLVI.

Of Pardons.

AS punifhments become more mild, clemency and pardon are lefs necef-fary. Happy the nation in which they will be confidered as dangerous! Clemency, which has often been deemed a fufficient fubftitute for every other virtue in fovereigns, fhould be excluded in a perfect legiflation, where punifhments are mild, and the pro-ceedings in criminal cafes regular and ex-peditious. This truth will feem cruel to
thofe

thofe who live in countries, where, from
the abfurdity of the laws, and the feverity
of punifhments, pardons, and the clemency
of the prince, are neceffary. It is indeed one
of the nobleft prerogatives of the throne,
but, at the fame time, a tacit difapprobation
of the laws. Clemency is a virtue which
belongs to the legiflator, and not to the executor of the laws; a virtue which ought to
fhine in the code, and not in private judg-
ment. To fhew mankind, that crimes are
fometimes pardoned, and that punifhment
is not the neceffary confequence, is to nou-
rifh the flattering hope of impunity, and
is the caufe of their confidering every punifhment inflicted as an act of injuftice and
oppreffion. The prince in pardoning, gives
up the public fecurity in favour of an individual, and, by his ill-judged benevolence,
proclaims a public act of impunity. Let,
then, the executors of the laws be inexorable, but let the legiflator be tender, indul-
gent and humane. He is a wife architect,
who erects his edifice on the foundation of
felf-love, and contrives, that the intereft of
the public fhall be the intereft of each indi-
                                    vidual;

vidual; who is not obliged by particular laws, and irregular proceedings, to separate the public good from that of individuals, and erect the image of public felicity on the basis of fear and distrust; but like a wise philosopher, he will permit his brethren to enjoy, in quiet, that small portion of happiness, which the immense system, established by the first cause, permits them to taste on this earth, which is but a point in the universe.

A SMALL crime is sometimes pardoned, if the person offended chuses to forgive the offender. This may be an act of good-nature and humanity, but it is contrary to the good of the public. For, although a private citizen may dispense with satisfaction for the injury he has received, he cannot remove the necessity of example. The right of punishing belongs not to any individual in particular, but to society in general, or the sovereign. He may renounce his own portion of this right, but cannot give up that of others.

N   CHAP.

C H A P. XLVII.

C O N C L U S I O N.

I CONCLUDE with this reflection, that the severity of punishments ought to be in proportion to the state of the nation. Among a people hardly yet emerged from barbarity, they should be most severe, as strong impressions are required; but in proportion as the minds of men become softened by their intercourse in society, the severity of punishments should be diminished, if it be intended, that the necessary relation between the object and the sensation should be maintained.

FROM what I have written results the following general theorem, of considerable utility, though not conformable to custom, the common legislator of nations.

That

That a puniſhment may not be an act of violence, of one, or of many againſt a private member of ſociety, it ſhould be public, immediate and neceſſary ; the leaſt poſſible in the caſe given ; proportioned to the crime, and determined by the laws.

Chapter 4.
JOHN ADAMS' COPY OF 1775, COMMENTS

One of the earliest translations is the one possessed by John Adams. It was the fourth of its kind, printed in London in 1775 by F. Newbery. In this book, the Coat of Arms of John Adams, stamped on the first page, bears the inscription in Latin: "Libertatem/Amicitiam/Retinebis/Et Fidem," which may be translated, "You will retain liberty, friendship, and faith." The name John Adams, appears beneath the oval Coat of Arms.

On the title page appears the inscription: "Thomas B. Adams. From his Father. 1800." This edition, republished in its entirety herewith, was, with another early edition in the orginal Italian, in the possesion of John Adams; and this edition which he bequeathed to his son Thomas is in the Rare Book Collection of the Boston Public Library.

It is interesting that in this edition the name of Voltaire appears both on the cover and on the title page of the book. The name of Beccaria appears only in the Preface of the Translator, reprinted from the first edition. The translator finds this somewhat peculiar. "With regard to the commentary, attributed to Mons. de Voltaire, my only authority for supposing it his, is the voice of the public, which indeed is the only authority we have for most of his works. Let those who are acquainted with the peculiarity of his manner judge for themselves." This peculiarity may also explain why the 1777 edition published in Charlestown, South Carolina, has the name of Voltaire and not that of Beccaria, aside from the fact that the American edition of 1777 appears to be a reprint of the London edition. It must also be noted that the same procedure was used for several early Italian editions.

The Commentary of Voltaire is divided into twenty-three chapters each dealing with a topic treated by Beccaria but expanded by Voltaire, who furnishes examples from situations taking place during his time, and making comparisons on how those situations were dealt with in France, in England, and in Rome at the time of the Empire.

It is difficult to say to what extent the Commentary served to promulgate Beccaria's thoughts, as there had already been several editions before Morellet's translation of the Italian into French. The fact that Beccaria's book became widely known under the name of Voltaire is significant at least in the promulgation of those ideas.

Voltaire's Commentary is not included in the present edition though it does form the second part of John Adams' copy.

It should further be noted that Adams' copy lacks the chapter, "To the Reader", which took the title of "Preface" in the early Italian editions. The chapter is translated herewith and various notes added. Also different from Beccaria's final edition is the order of the chapters and their subdivisions.

Chapter 5

BECCARIA, ON CRIMES AND PUNISHMENTS
(of John Adams)

> In all things, and especially in the most
> difficult ones, we cannot expect one to con-
> comitantly sow and reap the harvest; but we
> must first make preparations, and allow that
> things reach maturity little by little. (Bacon)

TO THE READER

The bulk of traditional legal opinoins which throughout
Europe have unfortunately been called laws are based on some
remnants of an ancient conquering people's laws that a prince
from Constantinople[1] had had compiled only about twelve centuries ago. Later, they were mixed with Longobardian rituals;
now they are gathered together into encyclopedic-type volumes
by private and little known interpreters of these laws. That our
very men committed to uphold the lives and fortunes of other
men should do so by obeying laws based on a single opinion
of a Carpzov[2] or on an ancient usage mentioned by a Claro[3], or
administer punishments with irate complacency as suggested
by a Farinaccio[4] is indeed a prevalent practice today as it is
pernicious. These laws — drainage of the most barbarous of
centuries, are examined in this book for that part that deals
with criminal procedure whose disorders I wish to expose to
those entrusted in securing the public's pursuit of happiness, in
a style which should keep away only the illiterate and the igno-
ramus. My simple inquiry of truth, and my freedom from public
opinions with which this book is written, are the result of the
sweet and enlightened manner in which I govern myself. The
great monarchs and the benefactors of humanity who rule over

us, should love the truth set forth herein with little fanatical vigor by this little known philosopher, reacting only against those who turn to force or to cunning industry and not to reason. The present disorders for the one who well examines all the circumstances, are the satire and the reproach of the past centuries and not of our century or of its legislators.

Therefore, let those who wish to honour me with their criticism begin to do so by understanding first the purpose of this work; for, far from trying to diminish legitimate authority, I wish to increase it more by the power of thinking than by that of force, especially if in the eyes of mankind authority is based on gentleness and on humanity. The misunderstood criticism[5] published against this book are based on confused notions; as a result, this criticism forces me to interrupt for a moment my arguments to the enlightened readers in order to close once and for all any access to the errors of a timid zeal, or to the calumnies of malicious envy.

Moral and political principles which regulate mankind come from three sources: revelation, natural law, and man-made conventions. In its main purpose, the first principle cannot be compared to the other two; but they resemble each other in this respect — they are conducive to our happiness. To consider the relationships of the last does not exclude those of the first two. On the other hand, though the first two are divine and immutable, they were changed by man's false religions and by man's arbitrary notions of vice and virtue that have existed in our corrupt minds. So it seems necessary to examine separately and without any other consideration that which is generated by pure human conventions, either expressed or supposed by common necessity and utility — the idea being that every faction and every moral system must necessarily come to some sort of agreement; for it will always be a praiseworthy enterprise to force the most obstinate and incredulous of men to conform to those principles that induce men to live in a society. There are, therefore, three distinct classes of virtue and of vice: religious, natural, and political. These three classes must never be in contradiction among themselves; but not all the consequences and the obligation derived from one may be derived from the others. Not everything demanded by revelation can be demanded by the natural law; nor anything demanded by the latter is demanded by the pure social law. But it is very important to separate that which results from the convention; that is, from the express or tacit agreements of men, because such is the limit of that force that can be legitimately exercised among men, without a special mandate of the Supreme Being. Therefore, the concept of political virtue can unblemishedly be called variable; the one of natural virtue would always be clear and manifest if it were not for the imbecility and passions of men that obscure it; and the one of religious virtue is always both one and constant because it is revealed immediately by God Himself and preserved by Him.

It would therefore be an error to attribute to those who speak of social conventions with their consequences principles contrary either to the natural law or to revelation, because the latter two do not enter into the discussion. It would further be an error for the one who, on speaking about a state of war before discussing the state of society, would give it the Hobbsian's sense[6] that the natural state precedes the political state, instead of taking it as a fact born out of the corruption of human nature and from the lack of an expressed sanction. It would be another error to blame a writer (as though he were committing a crime) who considers the emanations of the social contract, not admitting those very emanations prior to the contract itself.

Both divine and natural justice are their essence immutable and constant because the relation between two similar objects is always the same. But human or political justice, being but a relation between the action and the various states of the society, that relation can vary according as that action becomes necessary or useful to that society; nor can that relation be well discerned unless it is analyzed by the proper individuals in all its complicated and ever-changing relationships of civil combinations.[7] As soon as these principles — essentially distinct from one another are confused, there is no longer any hope to conduct logical arguments on public matters. It is up to the theologians to establish the boundaries of the just and the unjust, for that which deals with the intrinsic evil or goodness of the act: the establishment of the rapports of the just and the unjust — that is, the utility and the harm done to the society, belongs to the individual who deals in public matters; for, an object can never be prejudicial to another, because everyone can easily see how much pure political virtue must give way to the immutable virtue emanated by God.

Whosoever — I repeat — should wish to honor me with his criticism, should not begin by supposing that I stand for destructive principles of either virtue in general or of religion. I have already demonstrated that such are not my goals. And, instead of making me out an atheist or of being one having seditious tendencies, the critics should rather attempt to find me out a bad logician or a freshman politician. Do not tremble over each of the sentences that upholds human interests. The critic should convince me, on the other hand, either of the uselessness or of the political harm that could grow out of my principles, and demonstrate to me the advantages of traditional practices. I have given public testimony of my religious beliefs and of my submission to my soverigns with my answers to the "Notes and observations."[8] To answer to ulterior writings similar to those "Notes" would be superfluous. But whoever will write to me with that decency normally expected of honest men and of those enlightened ones who will dispense with my having to prove the first two principles, of whatever character they may be, the critic will find in me a man who will make every effort to answer all the questions. And above all, the critic will find in me a peaceful lover of truth.

Chapter 6.
NOTES AND COMMENTS ON
JOHN ADAMS' COFY.

1. Justinian I (483-565 AD), Byzantine Emperor whose jurists formulated the Justinian Code.

2. Benedict Carpzov (1595-1666), German jurist and author.

3. Emilio Claro (1525-1573), Italian jurist and author.

4. Prospero Farinacci (1554-1618), Italian jurist and author.

5. The allusion is to Angelo Fachinei, a monk from the island of Corfu, who confuted Beccaria's work with a diatribe of 1765 entitled *"Note e osservazioni sul libro Dei delitti e delle pene"*, on commission of the Venetian Senate which had proscribed Beccaria's book.

6. Beccaria refers to Thomas Hobbes (1588-1679), British philosopher who gave birth to Hobbism, a doctrine advocating submission on the part of the governed to the will of the governor in everything.

7. The Italian *"combinazione"* has the meaning of combining or of uniting two or more objects, numbers, etc., but without a pre-set order. Combinations, therefore, arise as various needs or necessities generate them.

8. The allusion is made to the diatribe of Fachinei. But it should be remembered that when the book was first published in France, it received a very mediocre response, especially by men such as D'Alembert. Only after the subsequent editions did the book receive unanimous approval, making a Voltaire admire Beccaria's book over Dante's *Divine Comedy*.

9. Beccaria implies that a good system of government is one wherein the legislators pass laws according to present and future needs of the populace and not wait until the particular situation arises to dictate the laws to the legislators. By planning for the present and for the future, man remains in charge

of the situation, thus avoiding becoming a victim of the situation.

10. Beccaria refers to the Industrial Revolution which began in England during the first half of the eighteenth century.

11. The challenge proposed by Beccaria is as significant today as it was during his life time. The same questions he raised concerning torture and capital punishment are being discussed today with tremendous concern.

12. Charles Louis de Secondat Montesquieu, French philosophical writer on government and on history. He is best known for his *Esprit des lois,* 1748, in which he shows his admiration for the English and the thoughts of Locke. Beccaria had the same admiration for England and its people.

13. As a result of Beccaria's book, the Italians did away with the death penalty. Instead, they have the system called "ergastolo" which is similar to but not the same as "death row." Once admitted or condemned to the "ergastolo," an individual has little hope of ever being anything other than a vegetable for the rest of his life. But in Beccaria's land, as well as in everyone else's land, the wealthy still succeed in having the laws on their sides.

14. Beccaria was also a great economist, having written on population and subsistence, a subject later treated by Malthus.

15. Observe that the word "right" is not in contradiction to the word "force"; but the first is rather a modification of the second; that is, the modification which is the most useful to the largest number. And for "justice," I mean nothing more than a necessary bond needed to keep together the particular interests which, without that bond, would become dispersed as in the primitive state of unsociability.

We need be careful not to attach to the word "justice" the idea of something real or concrete, such as a physical force or of an existing being; it is but a simple manner of conceiving of mankind — a manner which has infinite influence on the happiness of each man; and in no way less do I intend the other type of justice which is emanated by God, which has its immediate relationships with the punishments and with the recompenses of the future life (Beccaria).

16. Beccaria is in apparent contradiction to the later Romantics' view of the "noble" and "free" savage, and especially with Rouseau's observation that man is born free and everywhere he is in chains. Rousseau states that the fruits of the earth belong to all men and that the earth itself belongs to no one. Beccaria, on the other hand, implies that such fruits are not gratuitously given but that they are potentially in being and therefore available. To be able to enjoy any fruit, man must first avail himself of his intelligence in order to eventually enjoy it. But man alone cannot succeed, for the like reason that man cannot enjoy the liberty made useless by the uncertainty of not being able to conserve that liberty. Furthermore, Beccaria would infer that society was born when men created laws with which to live by, and not as Rousseau maintained that society was born when man claimed a lot of land for himself and other men accepted it to be so. Just laws, then, permit men not only to derive a livelihood from an otherwise sterile and neglected nature; but through them, men can enjoy the highest fruit which is derived from the ability to live together and free.

17. Only those crimes specified by the laws can be considered crimes.

18. The legislator and the judge play distinct roles; likewise, the prosecutor is distinct from the judge.

19. If each particular member is tied to his society, society is equally bound to each particular member through a contract which by its very nature is binding on both. This obligation, that comes down all the way from the throne to the last individual and is as binding on the most powerful as it is on the most miserable of individuals, means nothing more than this: it is to the interest of all that contracts that are useful to the greatest number of people be observed.

"Obligation" is one of those words used much more frequently in morality than it is in every other science; those words are but the abbreviated sign of a thinking process and not of an idea: try to find an idea in any of the words of "obligation," and you will not find one; reason it out, and you will understand and be understood as well (Beccaria).

20. Beccaria considers the act in reference to the given law; he does not believe in the spirit of the law or in the past interpretations of the same laws. Considering the spirit of the laws with its various interpretations gives various results for the same crime when the result should be one and the same. A good example of what happens when the spirit of the law with its interpretations and its localized consultations is this: a boy of African descent is burnt at the stake for allegedly stealing a chicken; a man of European descent is given house arrest for allegedly killing one hundred people.

21. Beccaria implies that the spirit of tyranny and that of letters do not go hand in hand. Were a tyrant to read his book, he would not understand it anyway, because any man who would understand what Beccaria is trying to say could not be a tyrant at the same time.

Many of Beccaria's ideas on the spirit of the law are derived from Vico, *Scienza nuova* 1725, and from Montesquie *Esprit des lois* 1748.

It is important to understand the emphasis Beccaria places on the correction of the laws in this chapter; the corrections also hinder the fatal freedom of debate from which grow arbitrary and venal controversies. In view of the fact that ours may have turned out to be a debating society, one should wonder how many venal and arbitrary debates may have arisen from outmoded laws that are still without corrections.

22. The laws need necessarily be obscure and complicated; otherwise how could the legislators, the judges, and the lawyers earn a living? Without them, how could the common man extricate a meaning from the verbiage?

23. Beccaria had reasons to be optimistic about his century. The French Revolution, after all, had not yet taken place.

24. Beccaria contends that while there are far too many crimes of passion which cannot be completely prevented, the laws that are passed on or for such crimes must be of the type that will prevent rather than contribute to them. Beccaria generally feels that too many laws generate rather than prevent crimes; this is due to the inequity, arbitrariness, and special interests written into those laws.

25. "Equality" not in the etimological sense of making equal or of "community," but rather in the unnatural sense of equality which bespeaks of the man-made distinctions of primitive and modern men.

There is also the obvious difference between the primitive savage of Beccaria whose human state is to be avoided at all costs and that of the "noble savage" of Rousseau to be imitated in order to save the dignity of nineteenth-century humanity.

26. In thinking about "honor," one has to recall the "pundonor" of the Spaniards especially common in the "capa y espada" comedies as well as in the tragedies; reflecting that part of society, the "pundonor" caused more victims than just about any other one element of the supposed insults to one's person.

27. This important axiom is being abused every day through rules and regulations of convenience. This principle is closely connected to the principles of the practice of secret accusations which, as is said in today's lingo, go under the forms of confidential statements. Two recent examples at a state university should suffice to demonstrate the abuse of Beccaria's sacred axiom: basing himself on confidential information, the Dean fired a faculty member. In a subsequent public inquiry, the individual concerned asked the Dean to reveal the information that was used for the decision. But the Dean who had refused to reveal the information in private, also refused to reveal it in public,

stating further that the individual concerned should have known the charges through intuition. In another situation, a second faculty member was fired by the Chancellor. When the individual asked to know the nature of the charges on which the decision was made, the Chancellor answered that he had followed procedures and that furthermore the information was confidential. As of this date, neither of the two individuals knows the extent of their innocence or guilt; and unless they are told what the charges are, the two will not be able to deny or verify them. The fact that institutions of higher learning practice this type of tyranny is all the worse because Beccaria's work is being taught at the same time.

28. Among the criminologists, the credibility of a witness increases according to the degree of greater atrocity of the crime. This is the sturdiest axiom dictated by the most cruel of imbecility: *"In atrocissimus leviores coniecturae sufficiunt, et licet judici jura transgredi."* Let us translate into our very language so that the Europeans might see one of the many and equally unreasonable dictums of those to whom, almost without knowing it, they are the objects. In the most atrocious of crimes (That is, in the least probable ones) the slightest conjectures are enough, and it gives the judge the right to go beyond the law. The practical absurdities of the legislation are often produced from fear, which is the principal source of human contradictions. The legislators (such are the jurisconsults authorized by chance to decide on everything, and to become — out of the venal and self-interested writers as they are — the arbiters and legislators of the fortunes of men) frightened by the condemnations of some innocent person, overloaded jurisprudence with excess formalities and exceptions, whose exact observance would allow unpunished anarchy to sit on the throne of justice. Frightened by some atrocious and difficult crimes to prove, they believed themselves to be under the necessity of getting around those very formalities that they themselves had established; and thus, now

248

with despotic impatience, now with feminine trepidation, they transformed the grave trials into a type of game in which chance and trickery became the protagonists (Beccaria).

29. The observation is very applicable especially today when so many individuals compete in becoming members of this or of that club or organization which, by their very nature — the so-called constitutionalized constitutions — assume the right to include or exclude at will any person or group whatever. As a result, an individual is often given membership more according to the degree of his pedigree than on his achievements.

30. American institutions — especially those of higher learning — practice and protect slander through written secret documents containing accusations kept in files in the form dossiers. The content of the dossier is kept from the individuals so they cannot challenge the decisions made on them. This system allows for individuals to make what are presented as legal and false statements, and those affected by the statements are not allowed to know the content and to challenge, if necessary, the veracity of such statements. Letters of recommendations also fall in the category of secret accusations. This practice makes an individual outright guilty, and the basic right of every individual being innocent until proven guilty, becomes both a rhetorical question and a mockery. This practice, which goes counter to several amendments of the Constitution, is being found even in state-run organizations and is supported by the tax dollar. In this situation, the individuals involved with secret accusations run the close risk of being treacherous — one because they practice as civilians what the military often do, and two because they use the people's own resources to practice a form of slander which goes against the very citizen who supports those institutions. This practice may also allow for a double standard such as is practiced by newspapers, which, on one hand try to publish secret materials and at the same time attempt to keep secret the persons involved. Regardless of the idealism

249

behind these practices, the end result is one and one only — it creates a society of informers who undermine everything they are supposed to stand for.

Slander is also practiced both verbally and in written form. By placing the stamp of "confidential" on slanderous statements, slander becomes very difficult to defeat, and it is found where one would not think likely to find it — at institutions of higher learning, and at the highest level of governments, as disclosed by Watergate.

31. Basic human and constitutional rights — be they of criminal involvement or of otherwise, man is innocent until proven guilty.

32. Obvious admiration of the English system.

33. Frederick William II 1744-97, king of Prussia 1786-97; German in politics, French in culture, anti-Machiavelli, he was a friend of Voltaire with whom he spent three years in the castle of Sans Souci.

34. This may be wishful thinking on the part of Beccaria in reference to our situation wherein we see every day the in-effectiveness of crime prevention. Few if any examples are gotten from successful prosecutions that may serve to deter others from committing more crimes, be they of passion or premeditated. Crime prevention are but words when one considers that our penal system makes criminals out of the non-criminals.

35. A practice not uncommon today: consider a city's revenue from the fines imposed on illegally parked cars. Without this revenue, many cities would go bankrupt. It is to be wondered whether the myriads of "no parking" signs are designed to attract clients rather than protect the parking rights of those same individuals.

36. "I swear to tell the truth, the whole truth, nothing but the truth, so help me God!"

37. The higher the position of responsibility, the higher or the stiffer the punishment when committing crimes. In Beccaria's

days, the nobles "got away with murder"; and, in contrast with our present-day situation, very little has changed, the practice still remaining.

38. Practically an impossibility today due to the available transportation and communication means which place every corner of the earth within the reach of every individual. Nevertheless, deportation is being used by practically every modern government.

39. Silla Lucius Cornelius, Roman politician and general 138-78 BC, introduced the first of the "spoils" system.

40. Empress Elizabeth of Russia 1709-1762, daughter of Peter the Great of the Romanov family. Having acceded to the throne through a *coup d'etat,* during her reign, 1741-1761, she did not allow capital punishment though she annexed Sweden to Russia and defeated Prussia. She colonized the steppes and promoted the University of Moscow. Elizabeth did all this while leading a very scandalous life of her own. She then was followed by Catherine, who continued in her footsteps both politically and privately.

41. Famous Roman names: Titus Flavius V., 39-81 A.D., had excellent qualities as governor; Marcus Aurelius Antoninus, 121-180, was often referred to as the "delight of mankind"; and Marcus Ulpius Traianus, 53-117, developed some very enlightened criteria of government. Contrary to Christianity, Traianus was moderate in the persecutions.

42. That the prison is a place of punishment is being argued all over the U.S. Those who automatically consider imprisonment as automatic punishment exclude the possibility of a prison being also a place for temporary detention.

43. Prescription from the Italian *"prescrizione"* which establishes the amount of time after which one loses the right to prosecute for a given crime; similar to our Statute of Limitations which defines the period during which a claim may be prosecuted.

44. This attraction is similar in many instances to force of gravity that moves the universe; because, like gravitation, it diminishes with the distances; and if gravity modifies all the movements of the celestial bodies, likewise that powerful attraction modifies almost all of the movements of the mind as long as it lasts; they are different in this respect, that gravity places itself on equilibrium with the obstacles, whereas the attraction of the sexes more or less gains force and vigor in proportion to the increase of the obstacles themselves (Beccaria).

45. Another obvious contrast on the origin of society to that of Rousseau's *Social Contract* published in 1762.

46. In view of the Bamboo and Iron curtains — not to speak of the Berlin Wall, we must proclaim Beccaria to be unfortunately wrong on this very important point.

47. When the boundaries of a country increase at a rate greater than its population, here luxury favors despotism because where there are fewer men, fewer industries, when industry is minor, poverty depends more on displays of the wealthy, and the unification of the oppressed against the oppressors is that much more difficult to materialize and therefore less feared, because, homages, offices, titles, and submissions that render the distance between the strong and the weak more noticeable, are more easily obtainable from the few than from the many, as men are more independent when they are large in number than when they are small in number. But where the population grows in greater proportion to the boundaries, luxury is opposed to despotism because luxury gives life to the industry and activity of men; and the needy offer too many pleasures and comforts to the wealthy, so that those ostentations which increase the opinion of dependence will find less and less room. Therefore, it can be observed that in those vast, weak, and sparsely populated nations, if there are no other motives for obstacles, ostentatious luxury prevails over that of comfort; but

in the more populated and less vast nations, the luxury of comfort always causes the luxury of ostentation to diminish (Beccaria).

48. Beccaria would argue that were Fidel Castro to take a firm hand — based on justice rather than on politics — there would not be the crime of hi-jacking; at the very least, this type of crime would not be so frequent.

49. Beccaria uses almost the same technique he used when talking about the nobility. By stating that he does not want to treat or talk about a particular point, he actually ends up by stating or criticizing the situation. There is no doubt that here he refers to the religious persecutions of both Catholic and Protestant Europe. Those Americans wishing to break away from the Constitution and the Superior Court's decision might reconsider in light of Beccaria's observations on the place of religious practices and ideas in public places.

50. In this respect, science was and has been harmful in that it has destroyed the fleeting object. Science has also reduced and restricted the scope of religion, especially in the area of miracles.

51. When opinions become damaging, it is symptomatic of a debating society.

52. Beccaria alludes to G. Vico, *Scienza Nuova,* 1725.

Chapter 7.
INFLUENCE OF ITALIAN COLONISTS ON THOSE AMERICANS RESPONSIBLE FOR THEIR COUNTRY'S INDEPENDENCE AND EVENTUAL GOVERNMENT STRUCTURE.

In a letter to Philip Mazzei, Benjamin Franklin expresses his delight over the fact that Mazzei, upon receipt of a copy of the 1776 DECLARATION OF INDEPENDENCE — directly from and in the handwriting of Jefferson — had made a translation into Italian and sent a copy to the Duke of Tuscany.

That Mazzei had made a translation of the final rendition of the 1776 DECLARATION is of very little importance, since the document was immediately translated and published in the various countries of Europe. But that Mazzei should have received a copy directly from Jefferson may be explained by the fact that Mazzei and Jefferson had been and were good friends. More than this, since Mazzei had written many articles and pamphlets on behalf of independence for America, and because he may have been more influential in stirring the colonists against the English tyranny than is otherwise known, Jefferson may have wanted to express his appreciation to Mazzei by sending him a personal copy.

Philip Mazzei, who came to Virginia by way of England in the late months of 1773, together with a Mrs. Martin and her daughter — Mazzei regretfully married her at a later date —, held many important positions from the time of his arrival in 1773 to the time he left for Europe in the fall of 1778 as an envoy of the State of Virginia with the purpose of raising funds and of gaining support for the united colonies. "Our cause is just. Our union is perfect. Our internal Resources are great, and if necessary foreign Assistance is undoubtedly attainable."

From 1773 to 1778, a most crucial period for the colonies, Mazzei became an elected official of the vestry. Commercially, he formed a company for the purpose of making wine and oil, and of introducing to the continent vines and other agricultural plants and silk. As a soldier he joined the Independent Company of Albermale, fighting against the British on behalf of Virginia, all the while writing several articles and pamphlets under the pen-name of "Furioso" during the years 1774-75 and publishing them in John Pinkney's *Virginia Gazette* (Mazzei, *Memoirs*, translation by H.R. Marraro, Columbia U. Press, N.Y. 1942).

This typical Italian traveler and adventurer of the eighteenth century, who went from Italy to Smyrna to England to North America to Poland to various other countries of Europe and back to North America and finally to Italy; a man who counted personal friends such as John, Richard, and Thomas Adams, Carlo Bellini, Benjamin Franklin, Patrick Henry, Lafayette, Thomas Jefferson, and George Washington; a man who on reading *On Crimes and Punishments* espoused Beccaria's utilitarian philosophy of the "felicità publica," that is, maximum happiness to the greatest number of people; a man who was as much against any pedigree hegemonies as he was against the establishment of religious monopolies, especially if backed by established governments: this man Mazzei, together with individuals the like of Jefferson and John Adams, directly and indirectly reduced Beccaria's "humane and wise treatise" to a system of laws that found their practical if not pragmatic framework in documents like the declarations of Causes and of Independence, and the Constitution of the United States with its Beccarian Bill of Rights.

During the crucial years of 1774-75 that saw the shaping process for what was going to be the future United States of America, in John Pinkney's GAZETTE, Mazzei was to publish the following thoughts:

To attain our goal it is necessary, my dear fellow-citizens to discuss the natural rights of man and the foundations of a free government . . .

All men are by nature equally free and independent. This equality is essential to the establishment of a liberal government. Every individual must be equal to every other in his natural rights. The division of society into ranks has always been and will always continue to be a very serious obstacle to the attainment of this end. . . . I repeat that a truly republican form of government cannot exist except where all men — from the very rich to the very poor — are perfectly equal in their natural rights. Fortunately, we are now free on this continent . . . Now when certain privileges are exercised by a portion of the inhabitants and denied to others, it is vain to hope for the establishment of a liberal and permanent government, unless the favored citizens are willing to relinquish their priviliges and stand on a footing of perfect equality with the rest of the inhabitants. Discrimination inevitably arouses envy and ill-feeling . . . Therefore, liberty will always be insecure and finally doomed to collapse. . . . Democracy, I mean representative democracy, which embraces all individuals in one simple body, without any distinction whatsoever, is certainly the only form of government under which a true and enduring liberty may be enjoyed. Unfortunately for mankind, this form of government has never existed. The sacred name of democracy has been abused by tumultuous governments built on false and unstable principles. . . . (*Memoirs*).

Much of Mazzei's work during this time involved research on the Constitution of England with the goal of finding out its many defects. But perhaps the greatest lesson that he imparted to the colonists was the Beccarian observation that enslavement of the mind on the part of the political and religious organizations is effected through the brainwashing techniques of thoughtless repetition of given phrases or words aimed at establishing desired truths through the use of quasi-principles corroborated by camouflaged logic. Thus, Mazzei tells in his memoirs that even "Jefferson was amazed at the defects of the English form of government when I pointed them out to him, saying that they had not even occurred to him."

As the result of Jefferson's admission, Mazzei goes on to explain why this had taken place and could still take place: "Ever since childhood, you have heard that it was the best possible type of government: you could see that it was such, in

256

comparison with the other governments of Europe; you must have read English authors who proved that it is far better than that of the Roman republic; finally, never dreaming of having to change it, you lacked the incentive to examine it in detail. But, provoked by the insolent way in which the English express themselves about other nations — 'They are 400 years behind the times' — I have examined it carefully and have noted the essential defects I have described to you." (*Memoirs*, p. 204). To this, Jefferson suggests that Mazzei go on with the research and publish his finding in the form of articles in order to bring "these defects to the attention of everyone." (See, "Camillus" at end of this chapter).

In the mind of Mazzei, however, publishing the findings was not enough. The newly discovered information had to be used to encourage and stimulate discussions among the people so as "to combat the prevailing prejudices and to point out saner principles." To this end, Mazzei diligently set about to engage in discussions with the goal of bringing out the "saner principles."

The saner principles involved the political and religious activities. The latter, in fact, was of paramount importance, knowing very well, as did Beccaria, that even the smallest religious jealousies could precipitate the type of dissension which would weaken the bonds of the constituted society and play into the hands of the enemy. Without losing sight of the various practices of the religious sects, and with complete tolerance for the faith of others, Mazzei made himself the watchdog against those who preached dependence on England and used their religious power as a means toward this end.

Jefferson, on being aware of this danger, sought Mazzei to help on this matter.

"Jefferson sought my opinion on many matters," says Mazzei in his *Memoirs*. And among the many matters, the most important was the religious issue, especially that which dealt with certain special rights reserved to the predominant Anglican denomination. "Its ministers could not bear being placed on an equal footing with those of other denominations and reduced to living on the voluntary contributions of their parishioners, after having been supported until then by the state." (*Memoirs*, p. 215.)

Edmund Pendleton attempted to discredit Mazzei by fabricating false accusations which he then secretly passed to the people. Mazzei was accused of "wishing to introduce popery and of . . . being in correspondence with the English ministry." On discovering the plot, Jefferson is reported to have remarked to Mazzei, "Pendleton will see that the shoe fits him."

On another occasion, Mazzei went to hear a Methodist from England preaching what turned out to be an underhanded sermon, to say the least. "When we arrived," explains Mazzei, "he had been speaking of the dangers which beset the soul through sudden death; then he mentioned how great that danger was in time of war and recalled to the minds of mothers and fathers their duty toward their children, namely, to remove them from danger.

"One could easily see the point of his sermon. As soon as he had descended from the pulpit, I ascended it and told him that, having listened to his evangelical doctrine, I hoped he would be so kind as to listen to mine. Although he said not a word, he showed that he was anxious to leave, but my friends told him in an authoritative manner that he must stay.

"I began by saying that the intention of the British government was made clearly manifest by the Boston blockade, by armed encounter which had taken place on the outskirts of that city, by our governor's conduct, by the landing of English troops at Hampton, and so on.

"Then I spoke of Lord Dartmouth, who had been made secretary of state, so that he might send his satellites to the colonies to preach the doctrine which we had heard from that minister, and by means of which our adversaries hoped to place a yoke around our necks, without the least opposition. But I predicted (turning to him) that they would make the trip in vain." (*Memoirs*, pp. 216-7).

It might be opportune to mention at this time that upon leaving Virginia on his mission to Europe, he took the following documents: Bill for Establishing Religious Freedom, a copy of which is at the end of this chapter, Bill on Crimes and Punishments, Bill on the Qualifications Requisite to Constitute a Citizen, and two bills on Public Establishment for Education.

Among the several Italians residing in the colonies at this time were the Paca families in Maryland — William Paca signed the Declaration of Independence of July 4, 1776 —, Philip Mazzei with his entourage of farmers and craftsmen, and Charles Bellini, who was one of the first teachers of modern languages in the Virginia colony. It should be no surprise, therefore, to learn of the possible influences of Italian thought on those Americans responsible for this country's independence and its eventual government structure.

As witnessed by Mazzei, the Italians were present from the very beginning of the stir, involving themselves in behalf of independence not only in deeds such as the military march to meet the British in which Mazzei with his two Tuscan friends took part, but also in the intellectual discussions that prepared the otherwise submissive colonists to take arms against their English tyrants.

It isn't at all strange, therefore — though it may still seem so even to serious American historians — to find a July 6, 1775, literal translation of the "Declaration of the Causes and Necessity for Taking Up Arms" as adopted by Congress.

Significant in the Italian version are the six entries which give additional information not found in the final edition adopted by Congress. Of less significance may be the structure, especially the paragraphing.

The Italian version has as many as five paragraph variations. Aside from these and together with the necessary connecting words which make the Italian version somewhat more fluid, the translation is very literal, and definitely done by someone who knew English and Italian rather well.

Although at this time it is not known who the translator or the scribe were, all indications would lead to Mazzei, and possibly to Charles Bellini. Should neither of these be the author, then the historians should look for other individuals of importance who may have had a role in this very first important document in which the Beccarian words of Honour, Justice, and Humanity prevail alongside those of Freedom and Liberty, a document which is both the foundation and cornerstone of the newly founded government of the United States of America.

Hazelton, in his *Declaration of Independence: Its History* (Dodd, Mead & Co.,) N.Y. 1906, reports on a comparison between certain rights of the English and American citizens, as written by "Camillus"* in a Pennsylvania newspaper:

ENGLAND

1. A tryal by a jury of his country, in all cases of life and property.
2. A tryal where the offence was committed.
3. A civil authority supreme over the military, and no standing army in time of peace kept up, but by the consent of the people.
4. The Judges independent of the Crown and people.
5. No tax or imposition laid, but by those who must partake of the burthen.
6. A free trade to all the world, except the East-Indies.
7. A free use and practice of all engines and other devices, for saving labour and promoting manufactures.
8. A right to petition the King, and all prosecutions and commitments therefor illegal.
9. Freedom of debate and proceedings in their legislative deliberations.
10. For redress of grievances, amending, strengthening and preserving the laws, parliaments to be held frequently.

AMERICA

1. A tryal by jury only in some cases, subjected in others to a single Judge, or a Board of Commissioners,
2. A tryal, if a Governor pleases, 3000 miles from the place where the offence was committed.
3. The military superior to the civil authority, and America obliged to contribute to the support of a standing army, kept up without and against its consent.
4. The Judges made independent of the people, but dependent on the Crown for the support and tenure of their commissions.

261

5. Taxes and impositions laid by those, who not only do not partake of the burthens, but who ease themselves by it.

6. A trade only to such places as Great-Britain shall permit.

7. The use only of such engines as Great-Britain has not prohibited.

8. Promoting and encouraging petitions to the King declared the highest presumption, and the legislative Assemblies of America dissolved therefor in 1768.

9. Assemblies dissolved, their legistative power suspended, for the free exercise of their reason and judgement, in their legislative capacity.

10. To prevent the redress of grievances, or representations tending thereto, Assemblies postponed for a great length of time, and prevented meeting in the most critical times.

* "Camillus" was the pen-name used by several individuals during this period. Camillus was the name of a Roman Emperor of about 365 B.C., responsible for the conquest of the Etruscans and for a new code of laws.

Declaration by the representatives of
the United colonies of America met in
General Congress in Philadelphia, which
sets forth the reasons and necessity of
their taking arms. Italian translation.

Dichiarazione
di Rappresentanti delle
Colonie unite dell' America
mericana adunati in
Congresso Generale in Fila-
delfia, che espone le ragioni
e la loro necessità di
prender l'armi...

1. Se fosse possibile per uomini ragionevoli di credere che il Divino Autore della nostra esistenza avesse
voluto che una parte del genere umano possedesse un assoluto illimitato
dominio sulle persone e sulla roba
delle altre / destinate dalla sua
infinita bontà e sapienza a portar un duro e pesante giogo, al quale
non fosse lecito di opporsi / gli
Abitanti di queste Colonie potrebbero almen pretendere dal Parlamento della Gran Brettagna
qualche prova dell'essere stata
concessa a Lui questa tremenda
autorità sopra di esse. E la
la reverenza dovuta al nostro gran
Creatore, i principj d'umanità
e il senso comune, convinceranno
chiunque rifletta su tal soggetto,

154

e Città di Londra, di Bristol e di
molte altre. Il Parlamento adoprò
un insidioso maneggio per suscitar
divisioni fra noi, per stabilire un
perpetuo incanto d'imposizioni, ove
una Colonia offrisse contro l'altra,
nessuna sappiendo qual somma potessi
redimersi, e così estorcere da noi
colla punta della baionetta le
incerte somme sufficiente a soddisfare,
se è possibile di soddisfare la rapacità dei Ministri; rilasciandoci la
miserabile indulgenza di raccogliere
a modo nostro il prescritto tributo.

Quai più rigide e umilianti condizioni potrebbero proscriversi da
vincitori inumani a conquistati
nemici? L'accettarle nella nostra
situazione sarebbe l'istesso che
meritarle.

Subito giunte le dette notizie
su questo Continente il General Gage
il quale l'anno scorso aveva preso e
fortificato la Città di Boston nella
Provincia del Golfo Massachusetts, ai
19 d'Aprile mandò fuori un grosso distaccamento, il quale non provocato
assaltò gli abitanti della detta Provincia al Borgo di Lexington, come apparisce dai deposti d'un gran numero di
persone, alcune delle quali erano uffiziali

5. La risoluzione del Parlamento, alla quale
queste reflessioni si riferiscono, dichiara che
ciascheduna Colonia debba erigere un
fondo per il sostegno del governo civile e
dei ministri di giustizia nel proprio
paese; che debba contribuire la sua proporzionata quota per la comun difesa dell'
Impero Britanno; che questa contribuzione
debba restare a disposizion del Parlamento:
e che se la somma offerta sarà creduta ade-
guata alle forze di detta Colonia; allora
il Parlamento non metterà altre imposizioni
su quella Colonia che quelle che tenderanno
a regolare il suo commercio.

A questo le Colonie hanno risposto
Ch'hanno sufficientemente preveduto al
mantenimento del loro proprio civile e dell'
amministrazion di giustizia; che il
Parlamento non può aver altre vedute
in questo affare che di moltiplicar cariche
inutili per poter più corrompere la
giustizia e il governo; e che finalmente
il Parlamento non ha alcun diritto de meco-
larsi in questi loro affari.

Che il monopolio del commercio delle
Colonie goduto dalla Granbrettagna monta

...soldati del detto distaccamento, ucci-
...tti abitanti e ne ferì molti altri
...di Là passò al Borgo di Concord, e
si gettò sopra una truppa di abitanti
dell'istessa Provincia, ne uccise e ne
ferì degli altri, fino a tanto che gli
Abitanti della Campagna adunati
al primo grido di questo barbaro attac-
lo forzarono a ritirarsi. 6. Le ostili-
cominciate nel detto modo dalle Trup-
Inglesi sono state dalle medesime
proseguite senza riguardo a Fede,
reputazione. Gli abitanti di Bosto-
confinati nella Città dal Generale
...endo entrati in trattato col medes-
per ottener la libertà, fu convenu-
che depositando le Loro Armi appre-
i Loro proprj magistrati, potesser-
uscire e prender seco gli altri Loro
effetti. Le armi furon depositate
Ma a dispetto dell'onore e della Fe-
...uta ai Trattati, che gl'istess-
...vagg.. stimano sacri, il Gover-
tore ordinò, che quelle Armi depos-
tate per doversi conservare per
...ettivi Padroni, fossero prese di
...n prese, ritenne la maggior
...arte degli abitanti nella Città

...ritirata ... considera... tra morti, feriti e prigionieri, ...
... chiamata fuga, e che ... dai due ...
... il ... nel suo manifesto non à scrupolo di parlar
... Truppe per evitare ...

... ricominciata;

Con umile speranza nella misericordia del supremo imperiale
Arbitro e Regolatore dell'uni-
verso, devotamente imploriamo la
sua Divina bontà a volerci felicemente condurre al fine di questa gran
causa, a disporre i nostri Avversarj
a riconciliarsi con condizioni ragionevoli, e conseguentemente
a sollevar l'Impero dalle calamità
d'una guerra civile.

Per ordine del Congresso
Giovanni Hancock Presidente
Legalizzato da Carlo Thomson Segretario

Filadelfia 6. Luglio 1775.

157

July 6, 1775, United States, Continental Congress

Declaration by the representatives of the United colonies of America met in General Congress in Philadelphia, which sets forth the reasons and necessity of their taking arms. Italian translation. (The above appears in typed form).

DICHIARAZIONE 1775 July 6

dei Rappresentanti delle Colonie unite dell'America settendrionale adunati in Congresso Generale in Filadelfia, che espone le ragioni della loro necessità di prender l'armi.

Se[1] fosse possibile per uomini ragionevoli di credere che il Divino Autore della nostra esistenza avesse voluto che una parte del genere umano possedesse un assoluto illimitato dominio sulle persone e sulla roba delle altre (destinate dalla sua infinita bontà e sapienza a portar un duro e pesante giogo, al quale non fosse lecito di opporsi) gli Abitanti di queste Colonie potrebbero almen pretendere dal Parlamento della Gran Brettagna qualche prova dell 'essere stata concessa a Lui questa tremenda autorità sopra di esse. Ma la reverenza dovuta al nostro gran Creatore, i principj d'umanità e il senso comune, convinceranno chiunque rifletta su tal soggetto, che il Governo fu istituito per la felicità dei Popoli, e che deve unicamente tendere a quel fine.

Il Corpo Legislativo della Gran Brettagna stimolato da una disordinata passione per un potere non solo ingiusto, ma che sa esser particolarmente condannato dalla Costituzione di quel Regno medesimo, disperando di ottener l'intento per mezzi, ove dovesse aversi riguardo alla verità, leggo, o diritto, à finalmente tentato di effettuare il suo barbaro ed impolitico disegno di mettere in servitù queste Colonie colla violenza, e (rinunziando al Tribunale della Ragione) ci à conseguentmente ridotii alla necessità di ricorrere ancor noi alle Armi. Ma per quanto acciecato sia dalla intemperata sete d'un dominio illimitato, per cui nulla si cura della giustizia e dell'opinione degli uomini, noi per altro ci crediamo tenuti per rispetto al restante del mondo, a far palese la giustizia della nostra Causa.

I nostri Progenitori abitanti dell'Isola della Gran Brettagna abbandonarono il paese natio per cercar' un'asilo alla libertà di governo e di coscienza su queste spiagge. A costo del loro sangue, con rischio de' loro Beni, senza il minimo aggravio del Paese dal quale si partirono, a forza d'incessanti fatiche e d'invincibil coraggio, riescì loro di stabilirsi nei remoti inospiti deserti d'America, pieni allora di numerose e agguerrite nazioni di barbari. Formarono con Patenti del Rè Governi muniti d'ogni poter legislativo, e fu stabilita un'amichevole corrispondenza tra le Colonie e il Regno, dal quale erano originante. I reciprochi vantaggj di questa unione divennero in breve tanto straordinarj da recarne stupore. Si conviene da tutti, che da ciò nacque il sorprendente accrescimento della ricchezza, forza, e Navigazione di quel Regno; e il Ministro[2] che tanto saviamente e fortunatamente resse il timone della Gran Brettagna nell'ultima guerra, dichiarò in publico, che queste Colonie l'abilitarono a trionfare de' suoi nemici: Verso la conclusione della guerra piacque al nostro Sovrano di cambiare il suo Consiglio: Da quel fatal momento gli affari dell'Impero Britanno cominciarono a entrare in confusione, e gradualmente cadendo dall'apice della gloriosa prosperità a cui erano stati elevati per le virtù e abilità d'un sol uomo,[3] son finalmente agitati da convulsioni che lo scuotono fino dai fondamenti. Il nuovo Ministero vedendo che i valorosi nemici della Gran Brettagna, quantunque spesso sconfitti, mostravano tuttavia la fronte, formò la sventurata risoluzione di far con Loro una pace precipitosa, e di soggiogar poi i suoi fedeli amici.

Queste Colonie furon credute in situazione tale da poterne ottener vittoria colla spada nel fodero, e da poterle mettere a sacco sotto un apparente diritto legale. La costante loro quieta e rispettosa condotta fin dai primi stabilimenti, i loro amichevoli zelanti e vantaggiosi servigj in tempo di guerra, benchè tanto recentemente e amplamente confessati nella più onorevol maniera dal defunto e dal regnante Monarca e dal Parlamento, non furon bastanti a difenderle dalle meditate innovazioni. Il Parlamento fù subornato a adottare un pernicioso progetto, e assumendo un nuovo potere sopra di esse, à dato nel corso di undici anni prove si chiare da non lasciare alcun dubbio della sua intenzione, e degli effetti che ne seguirebbero sottomettendocisi. Quantunque abbiamo sempre goduto l'esclusivo diritto di dispor del Nostro, è stato preteso di appropriarsi e di distribuire il nostro denaro senza il nostro consenso: Sono stati fatti statuti per estendere la giurisdizione delle Corti dell'Ammiragliato e Vice-Ammiragliato oltre gli antichi limiti; per privarci dell'antico inestimabile privilegio d'esser giudicati dai nostri Pari, tanto nelle Cause civili che Criminali; per sospendere la Legislazione d'una Colonia; per interdire il Commercio d'un'altra, e per cambiare dai fondamenti la forma del Governo istituito con Diploma e garantito da statuti della sua propria Legislazione solennemente confermati dalla Corona; per escludere gli uccisori dei Coloni dal giuridico processo, e in conseguenza dal gastigo; per erigere in una confinante Provincia, conquistata dalle unite forze della Gran Brettagna e d'America, un dispotismo pernicioso alla nostra stessa esistenza, e per aggravarci di Truppe in tempo di profonda pace. È stato fin decretato in Parlamento che i Coloni accusati di certi delitti debbano esser trasportati e giudicati in Inghilterra.

Ma perchè ripeter le nostre offese ad una ad una, quando il Parlamento è arrivato fino a decretare che a diritto di sottoporci a qualsivoglia legge a Lui piaccia d'imporci? E chi ci difenderebbe contro un sì enorme illimitato potere? Neppur'uno di quei che L'assumono è di nostra elezione, nè sottoposto alle nostre Leggi: ma al contrario sono essi tutti esenti dagli effetti di tali Leggi, e ogni imposizione sulle Colonie, quando il denaro non s'impiegasse per un oggetto diametralmente opposto a quel che chiaramente si vede, alleggerirebbe il Loro peso a proporzione di quel che aggravasse noi. Comprendemmo la miseria alla quale un tal dispotismo ci avrebbe ridotti. Per dieci Anni continovi assediammo il Trono come supplicanti, ma senza effetto. Si dissero le nostre ragioni al Parlamento nei termini più moderati e decenti. Ma il Ministero prevedendo bene che avremmo riguardati il suo oppressivo disegno da uomini liberi, mandò Flotte e Truppe per effettuarlo colla forza dell'Armi. Lo sdegno degli Ameri-

269

cani si risvegliò, è vero, ma fù lo sdegno di un popolo fedele e amico. Si adunò in Filadelfia ai cinque di settembre scorso un Congresso di Deputati delle Colonie unite. Fù risoluto di offrir nuovamente un'umile e rispettosa supplica al Rè, e anche esponnemmo il caso al Popolo della Gran Brettagna. Abbiamo messo in pratica ogni moderato e rispettoso metodo; siamo fino arrivati a sospendere il nostro Commercio con tutte L'altre parti dell' Impero Britanno per dimostrare che il nostro affetto per qualsiasi nazione del mondo non soppianterebbe in noi L'amor della libertà. Questo ci lusingavamo che avrebbe terminata la controversia. Ma posteriori eventi anno dimostrato quanto vana fosse la speranza di trovar moderazione nei nostri nemici. Molte minaccianti espressioni contro le Colonie furono inserite nella parlata del Ré; La nostra Supplica, quantunque ci fosse detto che era decente, che sua Maestà si era compiaciuta di riceverla benignamente e di prometter di esporla al suo Parlamento, fù gettata in ambedue Le Camere tra un ammasso di fogli Americani, e là negletta. I Pari e i Comuni nella Loro parlata al Rè nel mese di Febbraio dissero che una ribellione esisteva attualmente nella Provincia del Golfo Massachusetts, e che le persone che La suscitavano erano spallegiate e incoraggiate da illeciti rigiri e macchine convenute tra i sudditi di Sua Maestà in diverse altre Colonie, e che perciò supplicavano Sua Maestà a porre in opra il piu efficace metodo per mettere in vigore le Leggi e l'Autorità della suprema Legislazione. Poco dopo il Parlamento decretò che alcune Colonie non potessero commerciare coi Paesi esteri, nè fra di Loro; poi che alcune non potessero pescare nei mari vicini alle Loro Coste, da dove solevan ricavare il Loro mantenimento, e gran rinforzi di Navi da guerra e di truppe furono immediatamente mandati al General Gage.[4]

Inutili furono tutte le persuasioni, argomenti, ed eloquenza di un numero dei più illustri e più distinti Lordi e Comuni, che nobilmente e vigorosamente allegarono la giustizia della nostra causa per sospendere o almeno mitigare la rabbiosa furia con cui questi accumulati oltraggi e senza esempio, ci venivano scagliati. Egualmente inutile fù l'interposizione [del] la Città di Londra, di

Bristol e di molte altre. Il Parlamento adottò un insidioso maneggio per suscitar divisioni fra noi, per istabilire un perpetuo incanto d'imposizioni, ove una Colonia offerisse contro l'altra, nessuna sapendo qual somma potesse redimerla, e cosí estorcere da noi colla punta della bainetta le incerte somme sufficienti a soddisfare, se è possibile di soddisfare la rapacità dei Ministri,[5] rilasciandoci La miserabile indulgenza da raccogliere a modo nostro il prescritto tributo. Quai più rigide e umilianti condizioni potrebbero prescriversi da vincitori inumani a conquistati nemici? L'accettarle nella nostra situazione sarebbe L'istesso che meritarle.

Subito giunte le dette notizie su questo Continente il General Gage, il quale L'anno scorso aveva preso e fortificato la Città di Boston nella Provincia del Golfo Massachusetts, ai 19 d'Aprile mandò fuori un grosso distaccamento, il quale non provocato assaltò gli abitanti della detta Provincia al Borgo di Lexington, come apparisce dai deposti d'un gran numero di persone, alcune delle quali erano uffiziali e soldati del detto distaccamento, uccise otto abitanti e ne ferí molti altri. Di Là passò al Borgo di Concord, dove si gettò sopra una truppa di abitanti dell'istessa Provincia, ne uccise e ne ferí degli altri, fino a tanto che gli Abitanti della Campagna adunatisi al primo grido di questo barbaro attacco lo forzarono a ritirarsi.[6] Le ostilità cominciate nel detto modo dalle Truppe Inglesi sono state dalle medesime proseguite senza riguardo a Fede e reputazione. Gli abitanti di Boston, confinati nella Città dal Generale, essendo entrati in trattato col medesimo per ottener La libertà, fu convenuto che depositando le Loro Armi appresso i Loro proprj magistrati, potessero escire e prender seco gli altri Loro effetti. Le armi furon depositate. Ma a dispetto dell'onore e della Fede dovuta ai Trattati, che gl'istessi selvaggi stimano sacri, il Governatore ordinò, che quelle Armi depositate per doversi conservare per respettivi Padroni, fossero prese dai suoi soldati, ritenne la maggior parte degli abitanti nella Città, [e] obbligò i pochi ai quali fu permesso d'escire a lasciarvi i Loro piu valutabili effetti.

271

Questa perfidia à separato Le Mogli dai Mariti, i figli dai genitori, i vecchj e gl'infermi dagli amici e dai Parenti che vorrebbero assistergli e confortargli, ed à ridotto alla più deplorabil miseria quei che erano avvezzi a vivere in affluenza e splendore.

In oltre per emulare i Ministri suoi padroni, con un bando dei 12 Giugno, dopo inventate le più insulse falsità e calunnie contro gli Abitanti di queste Colonie, gli dichiara tutti ribelli e traditori, interdice il corso della giustizia, e vi sostituisce la legge marziale. Le sue Truppe ànno massacrato i nostri paesani; ànno bruciato Charles-Town oltre un numero considerabile di case in altri Luoghi; i Nostri Vascelli sono stati predati; i viveri intercetti, ed egli non risparmia nulla devastare e distruggere tutto ciò che può.

Abbiamo notizie certe che il Generale Carleton, Governatore del Canada, procura di sollevarci contro gli abitanti di quella Provincia e gl'Indiani: ed abbiamo troppa ragion di credere che sono stati fatti dei maneggi per risvegliar nemici domestici fra noi. Finalmente una parte di queste Colonie ora prova, e tutte son certe di provare, fin dove può arrivar la rabbia dei Ministri, Le complicate calamità di fuoco, ferro e fame. Siamo ridotti all'alternativa di scegliere o una cieca sommissione alla tirannide d'irritati Ministri, o resistenza colla forza. L'ultima è la nostra scelta. Abbiamo ponderate le conseguenze di questa contesa, e nulla ci comparisce tanto orribile quanto una volontaria schiavitù. L'onore, la giustizia, e L'umanità ci vietano di ceder vilmente quella libertà trasmessaci dai nostri bravi predecessori, e che i nostri innocenti Posteri ànno diritto di ricerer da noi. Non possiamo indurci all'infamia e al delitto di consegnar future generazioni a quello stato di miseria a cui sarebbero inevitabilmente ridotte, se noi codardamente gli tramandassimo ereditarie catene.

La nostra Causa è giusta. La nostra unione è perfetta. Le nostre risurse interne son grandi, e assistenza esterna può indubbiamente aversi quando sia necessaria.

Riconoschiamo come uno special contrassegno del favor

272

Divino che non gli sia piaciuto che noi fossimo chiamati a questa gran contesa fino a tanto che avessimo acquistate [le] forza presenti, fossimo esercitati [d'] operazioni di guerra, e possedessimo i mezzi di difenderci.

Col cuore fortificato da queste animanti riflessioni, davanti a Dio e al mondo solennemente Dichiaramo che senza riguardo a qualsivoglia rischio, L'armi le quali i nostri Nemici ci ànno forzato a prendere, le impiegheremo con costante fermezza e perseveranza per la conservazione della nostra libertà, esercitando al sommo quelle forze che al benefico Creatore è piaciuto di conferirci, essendo unanimemente risoluti di morir liberi piuttosto che viver in servitù.

E affinchè questa dichiarazione non disturbi gli animi de' nostri amici e compagni sudditi dell'istesso Impero, gli assicuriamo che non abbiamo intenzione di disciogliere quella unione che à si lungamente e tanto felicemente sussistito fra noi a la quale sinceramente desideriamo di veder restaurata. La necessità non ci à per anche ridotti a quel disperato passo, nè ad eccitare altre nazioni contro di Loro. Non abbiamo messo in piedi Armate coll'ambiziosa idea di separarci della Gran Brettagna, e d'istituire stati independenti. Non si combatte per gloria o per conquiste. Si espone al Mondo il remarcabile spettacolo di un Popolo assalito da non provocati nemici, senza la minima imputazione, e neppur sospetto di offesa. Essi vantano i Loro privilegj e la Loro cultura, e poi non offrono condizione più mite che servitù o morte.

Nella nostra propria terra natia, in difesa della libertà, nostra per diritto di nascita, e che abbiamo sempre goduta finchè non fù ultimamente violata, per proteggere i nostri Beni unicamente acquistati dall'industria dei nostri Progenitori e di noi medesimi, contro [la] violenza ultimamente dimostrataci, abbiamo prese le armi. Le deporremo quando gli aggressori cesseranno dalle loro ostilità, e che sia rimosso ogni [rischi] o che sian ricominciate, e [no] n prima.

Con umile speranza nella misericordia del supremo imparzial Giudice e Regolatore dell'universo, devotamente imploriamo la

273

Sua Divina bontà a volerci felicemente condurre al fine di questa gran contesa, a disporre i nostri Avversarj a riconciliarsi con condizioni ragionevoli, e conseguentemente a Sollevar L'Impero dalle calamità d'una guerra civile.

Per ordine del Congresso
Giovanni Hancock Presidente
Legalizzato da Carlo Thomson Segretario
Filadelfia 6. Luglio 1775

---

1) Le annotazioni sono del traduttore (The annotations are of the translator).

2) Il Famoso Mr. Pitt, ora conte di Chatham (The famous Mr. Pitt, now count of Chatham).

3) Il detto Mr. Pitt (The aformentioned Mr. Pitt).

4) Governatore della Provincia e Comandante di tutte le forze Britanne in America, allora come adesso fortificato in Boston, di dove non ardisce di escire in campo aperto. (Governor of the Province and Commandant of all the British forces in America, then as now fortified in Boston, from where he does not dare go out in the open field).

5) La risoluzione del Parlamento, alla quale queste reflessioni si referiscono, dichiara che ciascheduna Colonia debba erigere un fondo il sostegno del governo civile e dei ministri di giustizia nel proprio paese; che debba contribuire la sua proporzionata quota per la comun difesa dell Impero Britanno; che questa contribuzione debba restare a disposizione del Parlamento; e che se la somma offerta sarà creduta adequata alle forze di detta Colonia; allora il Parlamento non metterà altre imposizioni su quella Colonia che quella che tenderanno a regolare il suo commercio.

A questo le Colonie ànno risposto Che ànno sufficientemente provvisto per il mantenimento del loro governo civile e dett'amministrazion di giustizia; che un Parlamento non può aver'altre vedute in questo affare che di moltiplicar cariche inutili per poter poi corrompere e la giustizia e il governo; e che finalmente il Parlamento non à alcun diritto di mescolarsi in questi loro affari.

Che il manopolio del commercio delle Colonie goduto dalla Granbrettagna monta molto più della proporzione dovrebbero contribuire per la difesa comune; che se il Parlamento ne pensa diversamente renunzi al manopolio; si permetta alle Colonie il libero commercio con tutto il mondo come godono gli Abitanti della Granbrettagna, ed esse contribuiranno liberalmente la loro proporzione per la difesa comune; che in verità le Colonie senza riguardo a questa libertà che potevano per giustizia pretendere ànno finora contribuito per la difesa comune più della loro proporzione; e che di questo lo stesso Parlamento ne à convenuto, come può vedersi nei suoi giornali.

Che le sole Colonie posson giudicar qual proporzione dovrebbero contribuire, e per quali usi, che non possono ammettere che il Parlamento decida su questo senza rilasciare a sua disposizione tutti i loro beni; e che questo diritto goduto egualmente dal Parlemento e dai Corpi Legislativi delle Colonie di giudicare ognun per se è tanto essenziale per un governo libero, che una minima parte che uno ne cedesse all altro sarebbe una cessione del tutto.

Troppo ci vorrebbe a ripetere tutto ciò che è stato risposto, e tutto coll'istessa calma e moderazione come qui sopra si vede.

(The resolution of Parliament to which these reflections are referred, declares that each Colony must create a fund for the maintenance of the civil government and of the ministers of justice of one's own country; that it must contribute its proportionate quota for the common defense of the British Empire; that this contribution must be at the disposition of Parliament; and that the offered sum will be taken as adequate to the strength of that Colony; then Parliament will not place other impositions on that Colony other than those which will tend to regulate its commerce.

To this the Colonies have answered that they have sufficiently provided for the maintenance of their civil government and for its administration of justice; that a Parliament cannot have other sights on this matter other than that of multiplying useless charges in order to then corrupt both the justice and the government; and that finally Parliament does not have any right whatsoever to mix itself in these affairs of theirs.

That the commercial monoply of the Colonies enjoyed by Great Britain is greater than the proportion which they should contribute for the common defense; that if the Parliament should think differently, it should renounce to that monopoly; the Colonies should be permitted free commerce with the whole world in the manner enjoyed by the English, and they will contribute freely their proportion for the common defense; that in truth the Colonies without regard to this liberty that they could with justice pretend they have up to now contributed for the common defense more than their proportion; and that of this, the same Parliament has given its approval, as can be seen in their journals.

That only the Colonies can be the judges in determining what proportion they should contribute, and for what uses, that they cannot allow Parliament to decide on this without releasing to its own disposition all their goods; and that this right enjoyed equally by Parliament and by the Legislative bodies of the Colonies to judge for oneself is so essential for a free government, that a minimum part that one cedes to another would be like giving up altogether.

It would take too long to recount all that was answered, and all (that was answered) was done with the same calmness as seen above).

6) Questa ritirata con perdita considerabile tra morti, feriti e Prigionieri, fu di 20. miglia in 6. ore. Di questa che gli Americani non ànno chiamata fuga, e che fù preceduta dai due d (--) barbari attacchi a Lexington e Concord, il General Gage nel suo manifesto non à scrupolo di parlarne come d un contrassegno di moderazione e d'umanita delle sue Truppe per evitare lo spargimento del sangue.

(This retreat with considerable loss among dead, wounded and prisoners, was of 20 miles in six hours. Of this which the Americans have not termed flight, and that it was preceded by the two of (--) barbarous attacks on Lexington and Concord, General Gage in his manifest does not have any scruple in talking about it as a countersign of moderation and of humanity of his troops to avoid the spillage of blood). (On the manuscript, this note appears across the bottom of the page).

Chapter 10

ENGLISH TEXT OF DECLARATION, WITH NOTES

THE DECLARATION AS ADOPTED BY CONGRESS
[6 July 1775]

A DECLARATION *by the* REPRESENTATIVES *of the United Colonies of North-America, now met in Congress at Philadelphia, setting forth the Causes and Necessity of their taking up Arms.*

If it was possible for Men, who exercise their Reason to believe, that the Divine Author of our Existence intended a Part of the human Race to hold an absolute Property in, and an unbounded Power over others, marked out by his infinite Goodness and Wisdom, as the Objects of a legal Domination never rightfully resistible, however severe and oppressive, the Inhabitants of these Colonies might at least require from the Parliament of Great-Britain some Evidence, that this dreadful Authority over them has been granted to that Body. But a Reverence for our great Creator, Principles of Humanity, and the Dictates of Common Sense, must convince all those who reflect upon the Subject, that Government was instituted to promote the Welfare of Mankind, and ought to be administered for the Attainment of that End. The Legislature of Great-Britain, however, stimulated by an inordinate Passion for a Power not only unjustifiable, but which they know to be peculiarly reprobated by the very Constitution of that Kingdom, and desperate of Success in any Mode of Contest, where Regard should be had to Truth, Law, or Right, have at Length, deserting those, attempted to effect their cruel and impolitic Purpose of enslaving these Colonies by Violence, and have thereby *rendered it necessary for us to close with their last Appeal from Reason to Arms.* Yet, however blinded that Assembly may be, by their intemperate Rage for unlimited Domination, so to Slight Justice and the Opinion of

Mankind, we esteem ourselves bound by Obligations of Respect to the Rest of the World, to make known the Justice of our Cause.

Our Forefathers, Inhabitants of the Island of Great-Britain, left their Native Land, to seek on these Shores a Residence for civil and religious Freedom. At the Expence of their Blood, at the Hazard of their Fortunes, without the least Charge to the Country from which they removed, by unceasing Labour and an unconquerable Spirit, *they effected Settlements in the distant and inhospitable Wilds of America,* then filled with numerous and warlike Nations of Barbarians. Societies or Governments vested with perfect Legislatures, were formed under Charters from the Crown, and an harmonious Intercourse was established between the Colonies and the Kingdom from which they derived their Origin. The mutual Benefits of this Union became in a short Time so extraordinary, as to excite Astonishment. It is universally confessed, that the amazing Increase of the Wealth, Strength, and Navigation of the Realm, arose from this Source; and the Minister, who so wisely and successfully directed the Measures of Great-Britain in the late War, publicly declared, that these Colonies enabled her to triumph over her Enemies. Towards the Conclusion of that War, *it pleased our Sovereign to make a Change in his Counsels.* From that fatal Moment, the Affairs of the British Empire began to fall into Confusion, and gradually sliding from the Summit of glorious Prosperity to which they had been advanced by the Virtues and Abilities of one Man, are at length distracted by the Convulsions, that now shake it to its deepest Foundations. *The new Ministry finding the brave Foes of Britain, though frequently defeated, yet still contending, took up the unfortunate Idea of granting them a hasty Peace, and of then subduing her faithful Friends.*

These devoted Colonies were judged to be in such a State, as to present Victories without Bloodshed, and all the easy Emoluments of statuteable Plunder. The uninterrupted Tenor of their peaceable and respectful Behaviour from the Beginning of Colonization, their dutiful, zealous, and useful Services during the War, though so recently and amply acknowledged in the most honourable Manner by his Majesty, by the late King, and by Parliament, could not save them from the meditated Innovations. *Parliament was influenced to adopt the pernicious Project, and assuming a new Power over them, have in the Course of eleven Years given such decisive Specimens of the Spirit and Consequences attending this Power, as to leave no Doubt concerning the Effects of Acquiescence under it. They have undertaken to give and grant our Money without our Consent, though we have ever exercised an exclusive Right to dispose of our own Property; Statutes have been passed for extending the Jurisdiction of Courts of Admiralty and Vice-Admiralty beyond their ancient Limits; for depriving us of the accustomed and inestimable Privilege of Trial by Jury in Cases effecting both Life and Property;* for suspending the Legislature of one of the Colonies; *for interdicting all Commerce to the Capital of another; and for altering fundamentally the Form of Government established by Charter, and secured by Acts of its own Legislature solemnly confirmed by the Crown;* for exempting the "Murderers" of Colonists from legal Trial, and in Effect, from Punishment; *for erecting in a neighbouring Province, acquired by the joint Arms of Great-Britain and America, a Despotism dangerous to our very Existence;* and for quartering Soldiers upon the Colonists in Time of profound Peace. It has also been resolved in Parliament, that *Colonists charged with committing certain Offenses, shall be transported to England to be tried.*

But why should we enumerate our Injuries in detail? By one Statute it is declared, that Parliament can "of right make Laws to bind us in all Cases whatsoever." What is to defend us against so enormous, so unlimited a Power? Not a single Man of those who assume it, is chosen by us; or is subject to our Controul or Influence; but on the Contrary, they are all of them exempt from the Operation of such Laws, and an American Revenue, if not diverted from the ostensible Purposes for which it is raised, *would actually lighten their own Burdens in Proportion, as they increase ours.*[1] We saw the Misery to which such Despotism would reduce us. *We for ten Years incessantly and ineffectually besiege the Throne as Supplicants; we reasoned, we remonstrated with Parliament in the most mild and decent Language.*[2]

Administration sensible that we should regard these oppressive Measures as Freemen ought to do, sent over Fleets and Armies to enforce them. The Indignations of the Americans was roused, it is true; but it was the Indignation of a virtuous, loyal, and affectionate People. A Congress of Delegates from the United Colonies was assembled at Philadelphia, on the fifth Day of last September.[3] We resolved again to offer an humble and dutiful Petition to the King, and also addressed our Fellow Subjects of Great-Britain. *We have pursued every temperate, every respectful Measure; we have even proceeded to break off our Commercial Intercourse with our Fellow Subjects, as the last peaceable Admonition, that our Attachment to no Nation upon Earth should supplant our Attachment to Liberty. This, we flattered ourselves, was the ultimate Step of the Controversy: But subsequent Events have shewn, how vain was this Hope of finding Moderation in our Enemies.*[4]

Several threatening Expressions against the Colonies were inserted in His Majesty's Speech; our Petition, tho' we were told it was a Decent one, and that his Majesty had been pleased to receive it graciously, and to promise laying it before his Parliament, was huddled into both Houses among a Bundle of American Papers, and there neglected. The Lords and Commons in their Address, in the Month of February, said, that "a Rebellion at that Time actually existed within the Province of Massachusetts-Bay; and that those concerned in it, had been countenanced and encouraged by unlawful Combinations and Engagements, entered into by his Majesty's Subjects in several of the other Colonies; and therefore they besought his Majesty, that he would take the most effectual Measures to inforce due Obedience to the Laws and Authority of the Supreme Legislature." Soon after, the commercial Intercourse of whole Colonies, with foreign Countries, and with each other, was cut off by an Act of Parliament; by another, several of them were intirely prohibited from the Fisheries in the Seas near their Coasts, on which they always depended for their Sustenance; and large Re-inforcements of Ships and Troops were immediately sent over to General Gage.

Fruitless were all the entreaties, arguments, and eloquence of an Illustrious Band of the most distinguished Peers, and Commoners, who nobly and strenuously asserted the Justice of our Cause, to stay, or even to migrate the heedless fury with which these accumulated and unexampled Outrages were hurried on. Equally fruitless was the interference of the City of London, of Bristol, and many other respectable Towns in our Favour. Parliament adopted an insidious Manoeuvre calculated to divide us, to establish a perpetual Auction of Taxations where Colony should bid against Colony, all of them uninformed what Ransom would redeem their Lives; and thus to extort from us, the Point of the Bayonet, the unknown sums that should be sufficient to gratify, if possible to gratify, ministerial Rapacity, with the miserable indulgence left to us of raising, in our own Mode, the prescribed Tribute. What Terms more rigid and humiliating could have been dictated by remorseless Victors to conquered Enemies? In our circumstances to accept them, would be to deserve them.[5]

Soon after the Intelligence of these proceedings arrived on this Continent, General Gage, who in the course of the last Year had taken possession of the Town of Boston, in the Province of Massachusetts-Bay, and still occupied it as a Garrison, on the 19th day of April, sent out from that Place a large detachment of his Army, who made an unprovoked Assault on the Inhabitants of the said Province, at the Town of Lexington, as appears by the Affidavits of a great Number of Persons, some of whom were Officers and Soldiers of that detachment, murdered eight of the Inhabitants, and wounded many others. From thence the Troops proceeded in warlike Array to the Town of Concord where they set upon another Party of the Inhabitants of the same Province, killing several and wounding more, until compelled to retreat by the country People suddenly assembled to repel this cruel Aggression. Hostilities, thus commenced by the British Troops, have been since prosecuted by them without regard to Faith or Reputation. The Inhabitants of Boston being confined within that Town by the General their Governor, and having, in order to procure their dismission, entered into a Treaty with him, it was stipulated that the said Inhabitants having deposited their Arms with their own Magistrates, should have liberty to depart, taking with them their other Effects. They accordingly delivered up their Arms, but in open violation of Honour, in defiance of the obligation of Treaties, which even savage Nations esteemed sacred, the Governor ordered the Arms deposited as aforesaid, that they might be preserved for their owners, to be seized by a Body of Soldiers; detained the greatest part of the Inhabitants in the Town, and compelled the few who were permitted to retire, to leave their most valuable Effects behind.

By this perfidy Wives are separated from their Husbands, Children from their Parents, the aged and the sick from their Relations and Friends, who wish to attend and comfort them; and those who have been used to live in Plenty and even Elegance, are reduced to deplorable Distress.

The General, further emulating his ministerial Masters, by a Proclamation bearing date on the 12th day of June, after venting the grossest Falsehoods and Calumnies against the good People of these Colonies, proceeds to "declare them all, either

*by Name or Description, to be Rebels and Traitors, to super-
sede the course of the Common Law, and instead thereof to
publish and order the use and exercise of the Law Martial."
His Troops have butchered our Countrymen, have wantonly
burnt Charlestown, besides a considerable number of Houses
in other Places; our Ships and Vessels are seized; the necessary
supplies of Provisions are intercepted, and he is exerting his utmost Power to spread destruction and devastation around him.*

We have received certain Intelligence, that General Carleton, the Governor of Canada,[6] is instigating the People of that
Province and the Indians to fall upon us; and we have but too
much reason to apprehend, that Schemes have been formed to
excite domestic Enemies against us. In brief, a part of these
Colonies now feel, and all of them are sure of feeling, as far
as the Vengeance of Administration can inflict them, the complicated Calamities of Fire, Sword, and Famine. We are reduced
to the alternative of chusing an unconditional Submission to the
tyranny of irritated Ministers, or resistance by Force. The latter
is our choice. We have counted the cost of this contest, and find
nothing so dreadful as voluntary Slavery. Honour, Justice, and
Humanity, forbid us tamely to surrender that Freedom which
we received from our gallant Ancestors, and which our innocent
Posterity have a right to receive from us. We cannot endure
the infamy and guilt of resigning succeeding Generations to that
wretchedness which inevitably awaits them, if we basely entail
hereditary Bondage upon them.

Our cause is just. Our union is perfect.[7] Our internal Resources are great, and, if necessary, foreign Assistance is undoubtedly attainable. We gratefully acknowledge, as signal
Instances of the Divine Favour towards us, that his Providence
would not permit us to be called into this severe Controversy,
until we were grown up to our present strength, had been pre-
viously exercised in warlike Operation, and possessed of the
means of defending ourselves. With hearts fortified with these

animating Reflections, *we most solemnly, before God and the World, declare, that, exerting the utmost Energy of those Powers, which our beneficent Creator hath graciously bestowed upon us, the Arms we have been compelled by our Enemies to assume, we will, in defiance of every Hazard, with unabating Firmness and Perserverence, employ for the preservation of our Liberties;* being with one Mind resolved to die Freemen rather than to live Slaves.

Lest this Declaration should disquiet the Minds of our Friends and Fellow-Subjects in any part of the Empire, we assure them that we mean not to dissolve that Union which has so long and so happily subsisted between us, and which we sincerely wish to see restored. Necessity has not yet driven us into that desperate Measure, or induced us to excite any other Nation to War against them. We have not raised Armies with ambitious Designs of separating from Great-Britain, and establishing Independent States. *We fight not for Glory or for Conquest. We exhibit to Mankind the remarkable Spectacle of a People attacked by unprovoked Enemies, without any imputation or even suspicion of Offence.* They boast of their Privileges and Civilization, and yet proffer no milder Conditions than Servitude or Death.

In our own native Land, in defence of the Freedom that is our Birthright, and which we ever enjoyed till the late Violation of it — for the protection of our Property, acquired solely by the honest Industry of our fore-fathers and ourselves,[8] *against Violence actually offered, we have taken up Arms. We shall lay them down when Hostilities shall cease on the part of the Aggressors, and all danger of their being renewed shall be removed, and not before.*

With an humble Confidence in the Mercies of the supreme and impartial Judge and Ruler of the Universe, *we most devoutly implore his Divine Goodness to protect us happily through this great Conflict, to dispose our Adversaries to reconciliation on reasonable Terms, and thereby to relieve the Empire from the Calamities of civil War.*

284

NOTES ON THE DECLARATION OF CAUSES

1. Revenue diverted
2. Ten Years fruitless Remonstrance
3. Congress of Delegates
4. Petition to the King
5. Auction of Taxation
6. Instigation of Canada
7. Perfect Union of Colonies
8. Protection of Property

MONTVILLE TWP. PUBLIC LIBRARY
90 Horseneck Road
Montville, N.J. 07045